FAWLTY TOWERS

FAWLTY TOWERS

by John Cleese & Connie Booth

Contact Publications Limited

Book 2

Designed by The Small Back Room for
Contact Publications Limited
91 Clapham High Street, London SW4

ISBN 0 7088 1547 2

Printed in Great Britain by Redwood Burn Limited,
Trowbridge and Esher

CONTENTS

THE WEDDING

A TOUCH OF CLASS

THE GERMANS

FAWLTY TOWERS
PRODUCTION TEAM

Producer	John Howard Davies
Producer's Assistant	Angela Sharp
Designer	Peter Kindred
Sound	John Howell
Lighting	Geoff Shaw
	Ron Koplick
Production Assistant	Tony Guyan
Make-up	Jean Speak
Costumes	Mary Woods
Tape Editors	Pete Dunkley
	Chris Booth
	Derek Orman
Film Editor	Bob Rymer
Film Cameraman	Stan Speel
Music	Dennis Wilson
Vision Mixer	Bill Morton

THE WEDDING

CAST LIST

Basil Fawlty	John Cleese
Sybil Fawlty	Prunella Scales
Manuel	Andrew Sachs
Polly	Connie Booth
Major Gowen	Ballard Berkeley
Miss Tibbs	Gilly Flower
Miss Gatsby	Renee Roberts
Alan	Trevor Adams
Jean	April Walker
Mrs. Peignoir	Yvonne Gilan
Mr. Lloyd	Conrad Phillips
Rachel Lloyd	Diana King
Bar guest	Jay Neill

In the cocktail bar

It is about six o'clock in the evening. Sybil is at the bar, deep in conversation with a customer; a conversation which is punctuated by her familiar laugh. Basil crosses the bar and is addressed by Major Gowen.

The Major By jove, it's warm tonight isn't it Fawlty?

Basil It certainly is, Major, yes.

The Major Very warm, phew!

Basil Oh! Can I get you another drink?

The Major . . . Oh why not indeed? What a good idea.

At the bar, Sybil laughs.

Basil Always reminds me of somebody machine-gunning a seal.

The Major The heat?

Basil . . . . . . No, no, my wife's laugh.

Mrs. Peignoir enters. She is attractive and slightly flirtatious.

Basil (*with much charm*) Ah, Good evening, Mrs. Peignoir.

Mrs. Peignoir Good evening. Thank you for your map, it was so useful. I must congratulate you. I had no idea how charming Torquay was.

She is a person of the French persuasion.

Basil Enchanté. May I ask . . . did you find anything of interest?

Mrs. Peignoir Yes. A few pieces I liked very much and one . . .

Mrs. Peignoir Oh! I <u>had</u> to have it.

Basil Ah, formidable. I'm so pleased. May I introduce—Major Gowen, our longest standing resident—Mrs. Peignoir.

Mrs. Peignoir How do you do, Major?

The Major How do <u>you</u> do, madam.

Basil Mrs. Peignoir is an antique dealer. She's down here for a few days, sniffing around for dainty relics.

Sybil lets out a real cackle. Basil winces.

Basil (*to Mrs. Peignoir*) Please don't alarm yourself. That's only my wife laughing. I'm afraid her local finishing school was bombed.

Mrs. Peignoir Oh dear!

Basil No, no, not really, just a thought. Well now, what can I get you?

Mrs. Peignoir Do you have any Ricard?

Basil (*blankly*) I'm sorry?

Mrs. Peignoir Any Ricard.

Basil . . . We're <u>just</u> out of it I think.

Mrs. Peignoir A sherry then.

Basil But of course.

*Smiling and bowing, the perfect host
moves away, leaving the Major with Mrs. Peignoir.*

The Major Are you—by any chance
—French at all?

Mrs. Peignoir Yes I am.

The Major Good Lord!

*Basil has crossed to the bar. He
observes Sybil.*

Basil Enjoying yourself, dear?

*Sybil looks at him. He would like her to
lend a hand.*

Basil We haven't put any nuts in the bowls, have we?

Sybil Well I haven't, I don't know about you.

Basil Well I'll do it then, shall I?

Sybil That would be the simplest solution, dear.

Basil (*thinking of an even simpler solution*) Where's Manuel?

Sybil We've given him the evening off dear, it's his birthday.

Basil (*muttering to himself*) Well, how old is he? Two and a half?

*There is another hearty laugh from Sybil
and her customer. Basil cannot find any
nuts under the counter.*

Basil Excuse me, there are no nuts here, Sybil.

The customer No nuts!!!

Sybil You'll find them in the kitchen.

Basil Oh will I?

Sybil Well, if you can bear to tear yourself away from Mrs. Peignoir you will.

Collecting the two drinks, Basil takes them to Mrs. Peignoir and the Major, saying as he approaches . . .

Basil Did you ever see that film 'How To Murder Your Wife'?

The Major How to murder your wife?

Basil Yes, awfully good. I saw it six times.

He leaves them and goes towards the exit, in search of nuts.

Basil Very funny.

Basil Very, very funny.

*Sybil laughs. Basil leaves the bar echoing
Sybil's machine-gun laugh . . .*

In reception

*Still mimicking, Basil comes steaming
through the lobby, attracting the attention
of Misses Tibbs and Gatsby.*

Miss Tibbs Are you all right, Mr. Fawlty?

Basil What? Yes yes, thank you so much. Are you all right?

Miss Gatsby Yes.

Basil Good, good. Well we're all all right then.

*Basil goes into the kitchen giving one more
strange laugh.*

Miss Gatsby Must be the heat.

Miss Tibbs Yes, he is getting taller isn't he?

Miss Tibbs and Miss Gatsby make their way to the main doors, passing Polly and a young man entering the hotel arm in arm. Polly is carrying a sketch pad.

Polly I think I left it somewhere . . . hang on.

She goes behind reception, putting the pad down on the desk and looks around for a book she has mislaid.

Polly Here it is. See you tonight.

Basil Yes? A single for tonight is it?

Polly Er, no. Mr. Fawlty, may I introduce Richard Turner?

Basil (*who is not too broad-minded*) I'm sorry?

Polly He's a friend of mine.

Basil Oh, you know each other. Just passing through are you?

Polly (*giving Richard the book*) See you tonight.

Basil Oh, we've opened a library have we? Oh <u>nice</u>!

Richard leaves.

Basil Don't go on my account Mr. Turnip.

Polly I'm sorry Mr. Fawlty.

Basil Now look Polly . . .

Polly I was just saying 'Goodbye'. No-one was . . .

Basil What do you think this is, a massage parlour? We run a respectable, high class . . . Did I say something funny?

Polly (*who is trying not to laugh*) I'm sorry, no.

Basil No, no, obviously I've said something frightfully comic.

Polly No, it's the heat.

Basil Well so long as I amuse the staff, that's all I'm here for.

Polly (*taking the bowl of nuts*) I'll take these in.

Basil (*not deterred from his theme*) Oh Polly, I'm afraid we've decided to abandon the idea of the topless afternoon teas, so if you wouldn't mind changing before you go in where people might be trying to eat.

Polly I was just going to.

She starts to leave, but Basil has noticed the sketch pad.

Basil Polly, would you come back here a moment please?

Polly comes back.

Polly (*to herself*) I'm on form tonight. (*To Basil*) Yes Mr. Fawlty?

Basil These kind of drawings may be considered decent at Art School but will you please not leave them on display at reception.

Polly I'll put them away when I've got some clothes on.

She leaves. Basil begins to leaf through the drawings. They are evidently permissive.

Basil I mean really . . . Tch! <u>Caw</u>! . . . Oh <u>dear</u>! Really!

The telephone rings.

Basil (*answering it*) Hallo, Fawlty Titties. What? Yes, yes . . . oh it's you Audrey. Yes, yes, what? He's left you again, has he? . . . Oh dear . . . oh dear . . . Oh I'm so sorry (*he is not rivetted*) . . . how sad . . . hmm. Yes I'll tell her. (*He invents a distraction*). Oh hallo, Major. I'll be with you in a moment. (*To phone*) Yes, well I'll ask her to call . . . mmm . . . oh yes . . . well keep your pecker up . . . bye.

Basil rings off.

Basil (*to himself*) Dreadful woman.

*Basil puts a pile of papers on the floor
behind the desk. Thus Alan and Jean, an
attractive couple in their mid-twenties,
fail to see him as they enter the hotel.
They are laughing, cuddling and giggling.
Suddenly they become aware of Basil
looking at them . . .*

Alan Hallo . . . we've booked a room.

Basil Have you?

Alan A double room.

*Jean leans sexily on the counter. Basil looks
without approval.*

Alan Name of, ummm . . .

Basil One moment please. (*He looks deliberately for the register*)

Alan (*quietly*) That's a nice suit.

Basil What?

Alan Nothing.

Basil I thought you said something.

Alan No.

Jean giggles.

Basil (*to Jean*) Are you all right?

Jean Yes, thank you. (*Alan pinches her bottom and she squeaks*)

Basil Are we ready?

Alan I think <u>we</u> are!

Basil (*impatiently*) . . . Well, may I have your name please?

Alan Yes, it's er . . . Bruce.

Basil Mr. and Mrs. Bruce.

Alan That's it.

Jean Is it a double bed?

Basil I beg your pardon?

Jean Has our room got a double bed?

Basil A double bed?

Jean Yes.

Basil Well we've only got <u>one</u> double bed . . . I mean, do you want that?

Alan Very much indeed.

Basil Tch! (*Basil sighs heavily.*) Well I'll have to put you in 12 then.

Alan All right.

Basil Tch! Tch! (*He turns to get the key, muttering to himself*) I mean why didn't you—never mind . . .

Jean Does it have a breeze?

Basil Does it have a <u>breeze</u>?

Jean Is it airy?

Basil Well there's air in it.

Jean Oh, I think there's a letter for me.

Basil What?

Jean There's a letter for me. There.

Basil No there isn't.

Jean There. Jean Wilson.

Basil Jean Wilson. Is that you?

*Alan laughs nervously. He and Jean have
sensed that Basil, unlike most,
will be looking for trouble. Basil hands
the letter over. Then . . .*

Basil Now what's going on here . . .
You're not married, is that it?

Alan opens his mouth to speak.

    Basil I'm sorry, I can't give you a double room.

    Alan Oh look!

    Basil It's against the law.

    Alan What law?

    Basil The law of England. Nothing to do with me.

    Alan Nothing to do with you!

    Basil Nothing at all. I can give you two singles if you like but . . .
(*he busies himself*)

    Alan (*to Jean*) Shall we go somewhere else?

*Jean is unwilling to go elsewhere. She is
still leaning on the reception desk, her
elbows on some papers . . .*

    Basil Excuse me.

*He takes the papers away rudely. Mrs.
Peignoir appears and deposits her key on
the desk. She is very friendly. Basil isn't.*

    Mrs. Peignoir Well, there's my key, and now I'm off to paint the
town red.

    Basil (*curtly*) Thank you so much.

    Mrs. Peignoir (*slightly surprised*) Well . . . perhaps I'll see you
later this evening.

    Basil (*looking away*) Yes, my wife and I will be up till quite late
tonight. Thank you. Good day.

She leaves.

Alan (*to Jean*) I don't believe any of this.

Alan Two singles then please,
if it's all right with the police.

Basil Two singles. Certainly. Now . . .

Jean (*intimately*) Next to each other.

Basil Next to each other . . . Oh dear, we can't do that. What a
shame . . .

*Sybil bustles in at this point and begins
to take an interest . . .*

Sybil Good evening.

Alan and Jean Good evening.

Basil Um . . .

Sybil A double is it?

Jean Well, we'd like a double.

Basil Two singles dear.
(*pianissimissiamo*) Not married.

Sybil What?

Basil Nothing, dear. I'm dealing with it, dear.

Sybil Well 17 and 18 are free. (*To Alan and Jean*) You'd have to share a bath.

Basil Noooooo! Oh, Audrey called—(*quietly*) I'll handle it—and George has left her again.

Sybil Oh no.

Basil (*to Alan and Jean*) Now, there's one on the first floor and one right up at the top.

Sybil Shall I deal with this Basil?

Basil I'm dealing with it dear.

Sybil Do you mind sharing a bathroom?

Basil I was here first.

Sybil Well it's my turn now then.

Basil I fought in the Korean War you know. I killed four men . . .

He leaves huffily.

Sybil He was in the catering corps. He poisoned them.

In the office

Basil comes in, turns and listens at the door.
There is a knock at the other door.

Basil Yes? . . . Yes, who is it?

Manuel Is Manuel.

Basil What do you want?

Manuel Can I go now?

Basil I thought you'd gone.

Manuel Que?

Basil I thought you'd gone.

Manuel No, no I turned it off.

Basil What?

Manuel I turned it off.

Basil No, I said I thought . . . he creduto que . . . oh it doesn't matter.

Manuel Que?

Basil It doesn't matter.

Manuel . . . Oh. You think I gone!

Basil Yes.

Manuel No, no, I go now.

Basil Wonderful.

Manuel What? Is OK?

Basil Is OK.

Manuel Thank you.

More knocking on the door.

Basil Oh, what is it?

Manuel Before I go.

Basil (*opening the door*) Yes?

Manuel Is my birthday.

Basil Yes I know.

Manuel begins to read a prepared speech from a piece of paper.

Manuel I want to thank you for your beautiful present (*he is carrying a new umbrella*).

Basil Oh . . .

Manuel . . . and for your much kindness to me since I come here.

Basil Not at all, my pleasure.

Manuel (*persisting*) Since I came here from Spain, leaving my mother . . .

Basil Outside.

Manuel What?

Basil Outside.

Basil slams the door.

Basil Thank you.

Basil returns to listen at the other door.

Manuel's voice Since I came here from Spain, leaving my mother, my five brothers and four sisters . . .

Basil goes purposefully to Manuel's door.

Basil Give it to me.

He tears up the speech and shuts the door. Manuel hovers. Sybil enters.

Sybil Can I have it, Basil?

Basil What?

Sybil I want that key.

Basil I've only got the key to room 12 dear.

Sybil That's the one.

Basil What!!! Now look here Sybil . . .

Sybil (*very sharply*) Basil!

Basil thrusts the key at her, Sybil takes it and goes back into reception. Basil points threateningly . . .

Basil If you were my size . . .

He opens the door and hits Manuel.

In reception

Manuel has scurried in.

Sybil Here we are. Manuel, room 12 please.

Manuel Si, si.

Manuel takes the bags upstairs. Alan and Jean follow. Polly comes down the stairs.

Polly Jean!!

Jean Hello, Poll!

Polly What are you doing here?

Jean We couldn't get in at the Bellvue.

Polly Hello Alan!

Another old friend.

Jean It'll be fun. My parents are coming tomorrow.

Polly Here, I warned you!

Alan Yes, we've already met the famous Fawlty!

Polly Ssh! I'm not supposed to hob-nob.

She motions them upstairs and they follow.

Jean I like your outfit.

Polly I'll give you the pattern.

In the upstairs corridor

Jean Are you going to be at Fiona's wedding?

Polly I can't, but I'll be at the reception, in my very own Jean Wilson creation.

Jean I want you to try it on later.

Polly OK. How's that gorgeous stepfather?

Jean I haven't seen him for a month. He's been in Singapore.

Alan Blast! I forgot to get those batteries for my electric razor. Anywhere open now Polly?

Polly You might find a chemist.

Alan goes back towards reception. Manuel offers round the bedroom key.

Jean and Polly enter the bedroom. Manuel shrugs and tosses the key after them.

In reception

Alan approaches the desk, looking understandably apprehensive as he sees Basil on duty . . .

Alan Hello again.

Basil . . . Well?

Alan We managed to sort it out with your wife.

Basil I wouldn't know about that. Is there something you want?

Alan Well, I know it's a bit late but is there anywhere I can find a chemist's open?

Basil I beg your pardon.

Alan Is there anywhere I can find a chemist that's still open?

Basil I suppose you think this is funny, do you?

Alan Funny?

Basil Ha ha ha.

Alan No, I really want to know.

Basil Oh do you, well I don't. So far as I know all the chemists are shut. You'll just have to wait till tomorrow. Sorry.

Basil Bit of a blow I imagine.

Alan (*returning*) What?

Basil You heard. Is that all?

Alan Well . . .

Basil Yes?

Alan I don't suppose you've got a couple of . . .

Basil Now look!!

Basil Don't push your luck. I have a breaking point you know.

Alan I only want some batteries.

Basil . . . I don't believe it.

Alan What?

Basil (*to himself*) Batteries. (*To Alan*) Do you know something? You disgust me. I know what people like you get up to and I think its disgusting.

Alan What are you talking about? They're for an electric razor. I want to shave.

Basil Oh yes?

Alan Look! I haven't shaved today. See?

Alan shows Basil his stubbly chin.

Basil An electric razor, eh?

Alan Right.

Basil . . . Well, I was referring to that when I said it was disgusting . . . It is of course <u>disgusting</u> that you haven't shaved, but understandable. I mean sometimes I don't shave and that's <u>disgusting</u> too, so I will have a razor sent up to your room, thank you very much, goodnight.

He leaves. Alan looks bewildered.

In the office

In the Fawltys' bedroom

Sybil Oh dear . . . he hasn't . . . ooh! I know . . . he doesn't deserve you, Audrey, he really doesn't . . . exactly . . . I know you have . . . I know . . . I <u>know</u> . . . oh I <u>know</u> . . .

Basil Are you going to go on like that all night?

Sybil What was that, Audrey? . . . oh I know . . . I <u>know</u>.

Basil Well why's she <u>telling</u> you then?

Sybil I understand, dear. I really do.

Basil Oh I can't stand it any more. I'll go and clean the roof or something.

In the distance the front doorbell rings.

Basil Ah! There's the front doorbell. Somebody's got back late.

Sybil (*ignoring Basil completely*) Yes . . . yes . . .

Basil I expect they forgot to get a pass key.

Sybil . . . Oh I <u>know</u>.

Basil Somebody'd better go and let them in.

Sybil . . . Yes! . . .

Basil I'll go, shall I? (*He nods several times*).

Sybil . . . Mmmmm . . .

Basil Yes I agree. Right. I'll go.

He gets out of bed and puts on his dressing gown. The bell goes again.

> **Basil** You know who that is, don't you? That's your pair. The Karma Sutra set. Good evening, welcome to Fawlty Towers Knocking Shops Limited . . .

He storms out, slamming the door.

> **Sybil** . . . No dear, it's only Basil . . .

In reception

It is very dark. Basil comes crossly down the stairs. The bell rings again.

> **Basil** I'm coming! I'm coming!

He hurries to the door, unlocks it and throws it open, saying angrily . . .

> **Basil** I suppose you know what time it is?

But it is Mrs. Peignoir, who comes in slightly and delightfully tipsy.

> **Mrs. Peignoir** Oh Mr. Fawlty, I'm so sorry.

Basil (*immediately oozing charm*)
It's only a quarter past eleven.

Mrs. Peignoir Oh, I got you out of your bed.

Basil Oh, not at all, I had a few little jobs to do and . . .

Mrs. Peignoir Oh, you're so kind.

Basil Oh well . . .

Mrs. Peignoir Oh, I had just a lovely evening!

Basil Did you? Oh, how very nice!

Mrs. Peignoir I saw some old friends I hadn't seen for years and I had a little bit too much to drink I'm afraid. (*She giggles sweetly*)

Basil Oh no, I mean, what's life for if you can't get a bit . . .er . . .

Mrs. Peignoir Blotto?

Basil Well, hardly blotto.

Mrs. Peignoir You're a very charming man, Mr. Fawlty.

Basil Oh well, one does one's best.

Mrs. Peignoir I hope Mrs. Fawlty appreciates how lucky she is.

Basil No, I think probably not in fact.

Mrs. Peignoir Oh!

She has dropped her purse. Basil is at once on his knees to recover it.

Basil Oh please allow me. Ah, here it is.

But in his anxiety to help he collides with the unsteady Mrs. Peignoir who falls onto his back. Alan and Jean come in.

Basil Ah there you are! Do come in.

Basil Well what a coincidence. Sorry, sorry.

Alan I'm awfully sorry, but we didn't realise . . .

Basil begins to explain loudly.

Basil No, it was quite extraordinary, the bell went just a moment or two ago and I thought to myself, I expect that'll be Alan and, er and down I came and lo and behold it wasn't you at all it was Mrs. Peignoir —Have you met?—Alan and . . . er . . . this is Mrs. Peignoir, she's an antique dealer you know, she deals in antiques. She's not frightfully old or anything, ha ha ha. And so I let her in not ten seconds ago, hardly five, hardly time to say good evening. Drops her things—just like that—so down I go and over she goes, ha ha ha, and bless my soul there you are and well there we are, it's getting on, golly, is that the time? I was thinking it was a quarter past ten, so can't stand around chatting all day. My God! Got to get an early night, up in the morning bright and early, so I'll wish you all a very good night. Goodbye.

*He disappears rapidly up the stairs
leaving the other three behind.*

Alan (*to Mrs. Peignoir*) Are you all right?

Mrs. Peignoir Oh yes thank you. Bonsoir.

Alan Goodnight Jean. I'll just make that call now.

Jean Don't be too long.

She follows Mrs. Peignoir upstairs.

In the Fawltys' bedroom

*Sybil is now off the phone, back into her
magazine and testing chocolates. Basil
comes in yawning noisily.*

Sybil . . . Well?

Basil . . . Hmmmm?

Sybil Who was it?

Basil It was your er . . . your pair . . . Huh! Caw!

*Basil gets back into bed. From outside the
door . . .*

Mrs. Peignoir's voice Bon nuit.

Basil Oh and that . . . that woman . . . er?

Sybil Mrs. Peignoir.

Basil Oh something like that, yes . . .

Mrs. Peignoir's voice Dormez bien, Monsieur Fawlty.

*Another long pause. Basil's discomfort
grows. He changes the subject.*

Basil How's Audrey?

Sybil She's in a terrible state.

Basil (*absently*) Good. Good.

There is a knock at the door. Basil starts, looks at the door and then immediately continues reading with tremendous concentration. The knock is repeated. Sybil is looking at Basil. Basil looks back at her. Suddenly he says very loudly . . .

Basil Sybil! I think there's someone at the door.

Sybil Why are you shouting Basil?

Basil (*just as loudly*) Was I shouting? Sorry Sybil!

He climbs out of bed and puts on his dressing gown again. He is totally unnerved.

Basil Well, I'd better see who that is then, shall I Sybil? I expect it's some key who couldn't find the guest to their room or some innocent explanation like that.

Basil Ready Sybil?

Sybil (*somewhat puzzled*) Yes, I'm ready, Basil.

Basil Right. Here we go then.

With a big gesture he opens the door about an inch. As he obviously can't see anything he opens the door wider.

Basil Hallo?

Manuel jumps out.

Manuel Olé!

Manuel <u>Poor</u> Mr. Fawlty!

Basil Ohhhh!

Manuel Oh Mr. Fawlty, I so sorry.

Sybil's voice Are you all right Basil?

Basil No I'm dying dear, but don't get out of bed.

Manuel I hurt you but you wonderful, give me such beautiful present.

Basil You're drunk Manuel.

Manuel No, is beautiful. Is my first one. Thank you, thank . . .

Basil moans.

Manuel Oh sorry, please. You wonderful man. I love you.

Manuel You so kind. I love you. I love you. I love you.

Sybil's voice Basil, I'm trying to read in here.

Alan hurries off, shaking his head.

Manuel Since I came here from Spain leaving my five mothers and four aunties . . .

In the dining room

Polly is serving the Major and as she moves away Basil appears from the kitchen. He approaches Mrs. Peignoir's table.

> **Basil** Et maintenant. Un peu de café??

> **Mrs. Peignoir** Ah, oui, s'il vous plaît. Café au lait.

> **Basil** Café what?

> **Mrs. Peignoir** Au lait.

> **Basil** Ah! Café . . . Olé!

Mrs. Peignoir laughs delightedly. Basil looks slightly thrown.

Manuel now appears carrying two cups of coffee. He sways towards the table occupied by Alan and Jean. He is looking terrible and the cups shake as he walks.

He gets them down on the table, spilling some of the contents. He wipes his brow, attempts to clean up the slop but is overcome and totters back into the kitchen aided by Polly.

Basil delivers a cup of coffee to Mrs. Peignoir.

Basil There we are. Voila sommes nous. Café pour vous.

Mrs. Peignoir Vous? Pas pour toi?

Basil No, I'll probably have one later.

Mrs. Peignoir (*laughs gaily*) Oh, that's very funny!

Basil Oh hah! Good. Good.

Mrs. Peignoir Oh Mr. Fawlty, I forget, the window in my bedroom I'm not able to open it . . . er . . . could you . . .?

Basil I'll pop up and fix it, certainly.

Basil walks away. Manuel now appears carrying two plates of food. He catches sight of them, which has a bad effect.

Basil Manuel?

Manuel Is terrible.

Basil Manuel, would you go in the kitchen please.

Manuel I can't.

Basil Manuel! go to the kitchen immediately.

Manuel Oh no, no.

Basil Come on Manuel.

Manuel No no.

Manuel lies inert.

Manuel Please. I die here. Please.

Basil Sorry about this. He's been working awfully hard recently.

Polly Mr. Fawlty, can I help?

Basil I can handle this on my own,
thank you Polly.

Alan They're at it again.

Basil I beg your pardon?

Alan Oh, nothing.

Basil I thought you said something.

Alan No no. Carry on.

Basil picks Manuel up and leaves.

Basil Get on with your meals!

In reception

Two newcomers, the Lloyds, are at the desk.
Sybil is dealing with them.

Sybil Thank you Mr. Lloyd. This is just for tonight isn't it?

Mr. Lloyd That's right.

Sybil Will you be taking lunch?

Mr. Lloyd We haven't got time I'm afraid, we've got this wedding at half past two . . .

Mr. Lloyd Would it be possible to have some sandwiches sent up to our room?

Sybil Certainly. Here's the key. I'll have your bags brought up in a moment.

Mr. Lloyd Thank you.

Mrs. Lloyd Could I possibly make a call?

Sybil Of course. Please use that phone there.

Mr. Lloyd leaves the desk and goes up the stairs taking his briefcase. Mrs. Lloyd starts dialling her number as Sybil goes into the kitchen saying . . .

Sybil Would you like coffee with the sandwiches?

Mrs. Lloyd Oh thank you, yes.

Sybil disappears. The dining room door opens and Alan and Jean emerge. Jean embraces Mrs. Lloyd affectionately.

Jean Mum!

Mrs. Lloyd Hallo darling, hallo Alan.

Alan Hallo Rachel.

Jean Where's Philip? Did he have a good trip?

Mrs. Lloyd Marvellous. He's upstairs. (*To phone*) Oh hallo, could I speak to Mrs. Brice please?

Jean See you in a moment.

She skips off upstairs. Alan returns to the dining room.

Alan I'll just finish my breakfast!

At this moment Basil comes out of the dining room with Sybil who gestures towards the cases.

Basil Well, where's the key?

Sybil He's already taken it up Basil.

Basil All right.

Mrs. Lloyd (*to phone*) Oh Anne. Rachel Lloyd here . . . hallo . . . how's everything?

Basil I'm going to take your cases upstairs.

Mrs. Lloyd (*to phone*) Oh yes, I <u>know</u> . . .

In the upstairs corridor and rooms

Basil takes the cases and carries them upstairs at a run. He hurries to the Lloyd's room.

In the Lloyd's room

Basil Sybil! Sybil!

In reception

Basil comes down the stairs and sees Mrs. Lloyd coming towards him. Basil must protect her from the goings-on in her room.

Basil Ah!...Hello!

Mrs. Lloyd Hallo.

Basil It's Mrs. Lloyd isn't it?

Mrs. Lloyd That's right.

Basil Ah, how do you do. Fawlty. Basil Fawlty.

They shake hands.

Mrs. Lloyd How do you do.

Basil Oh, pretty well really. Can't complain. Ha ha ha.

Mrs. Lloyd Good.

Mrs. Lloyd does not understand this odd exchange, which gets stranger . . .

Basil Well . . . hah! (*he indicates the door leading to the kitchen*) We . . . er . . . had this door knocked through recently . . . made rather a good job of it, don't you think?

Mrs. Lloyd Yes, yes very nice.

Basil Oh yes, beautiful, it's changed our lives really. We don't have to do the hundred yards through there and back again now, we can just open it . . . oh dear, it's not working as well as it usually does, ha ha ha . . . and go right in.

Basil demonstrates opening the door, going through it, and re-emerging.

Basil Just like that, it's marvellous. It's simple but effective. Would you like to have a go, see the kitchen and . . .

Mrs. Lloyd Well, I'd love to one day, but I really ought to be getting upstairs. See you later perhaps . . .

*She makes to leave. Basil suddenly grabs
his thigh . . .*

Basil Aaaargh!

Mrs. Lloyd turns round.

Basil Oooooh!

Mrs. Lloyd Are you all right?

Basil Bit of trouble with the old leg. I'd better just sit down in here a
minute.

*Basil backs into the kitchen. Mrs. Lloyd
follows uncertainly.*

Basil Bit of shrapnel. Korean War. Still in there. Oh dear!

In the kitchen

*Basil makes for the laundry basket, and sits
down, holding his thigh.*

Mrs. Lloyd Can't they get it out?

Basil Too deep. Too deep. Aaaaaagh! . . . Well, this is the, kitchen as you can see . . .

Mrs. Lloyd What?

Basil The kitchen . . . Agh! . . . Yes we had it plastered about five years ago and . . .

Basil Oh, don't worry about him he's just having a lie down. He's Spanish. From Barcelona you know. Sort of siesta. But he's fine.

He opens the lid to show Manuel is fine. Manuel groans terribly. Basil closes the lid.

Basil It was his birthday yesterday . . . So anyway, we got a few cracks up there but nothing serious so . . . aaah!

Basil So, as I say, it's not the Sistine Chapel but we're very happy with it.

*At this moment Jean passes the door and
Basil sees her. He gets up and stands in the
doorway.*

    Mrs. Lloyd Are you sure he's all right?

    Basil What? Oh yes he's fine.

Manuel groans again.

    Mrs. Lloyd But he's groaning.

    Basil Is he, is he?

    Mrs. Lloyd Can't you hear?

More groans.

    Basil So he is. Listen, I've just remembered I left your suitcases
outside your room, I left them just outside, by mistake, so I'll just go
and put them inside. I don't know if there's anything else you'd like
to see . . .

    Mrs. Lloyd No but . . . (*she looks at Manuel*)

    Basil Oh don't worry about him, my wife'll see to that. Sybil! Well
shall we? Come along, come along.

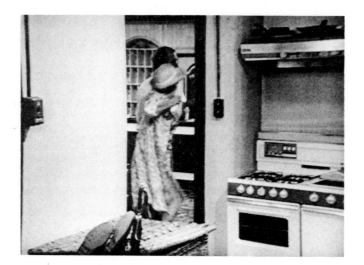

In the Lloyds' bedroom

*Mr. Lloyd is looking in his briefcase.
There is a knock at the door.*

    Mr. Lloyd Come in.

Polly comes in with tray.

    Polly Your sandwiches, Mr. Lloyd.

Mr. Lloyd Polly!!

Polly Hello!

Mr. Lloyd How are you?

Polly Fantastic.

Mr. Lloyd It's so good to see you.

Polly You're still gorgeous.

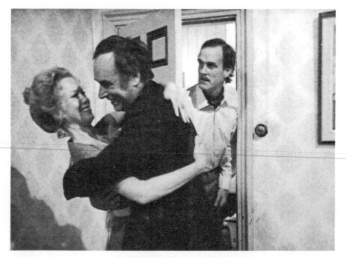

Once again Basil has to protect Mrs. Lloyd . . .

Mrs. Lloyd Is anything the matter?

Basil Mrs. Lloyd . . . er . . . may I have a word with you?

Mrs. Lloyd You are.

Basil (*thinking furiously*) Yes, quite. I'm afraid there's something that I need to explain.

Mrs. Lloyd Well?

Basil opens the door of the adjacent room.

Basil Could we go in here?

Mrs. Lloyd Is it absolutely necessary?

Basil I'm afraid it is.

Bewildered and thoroughly disconcerted, she follows Basil into the room.

In the other bedroom

Basil Mrs. Lloyd, I'm so sorry . . . but this is a much nicer room . . . than the one we've given you.

Mrs. Lloyd (*almost incoherent*) Wha . . .

Basil I was saying that I was sorry that this room is so much nicer than yours . . . and I wanted to show it to you . . . and to apologise . . . in case you found out about it later and got rather cross.

Mrs. Lloyd backs away a little.

Basil Now, the point is, um . . . the point is . . . if it turns out you don't like your room we could always move you in here, but I don't think it's worth doing yet, until you've definitely decided that you don't like the other one as much as this one, and then we can sort of sit down round a table, discuss it, chew it over and . . .

He observes Polly passing the door.

Basil And then it will be a piece of cake. Bob's your uncle. OK? Fine.

Basil hurriedly ushers Mrs. Lloyd back to her room.

Mr. Lloyd Oh thank you, thank you very much. (*To his wife*) Ah, I wondered where you were darling.

Basil gives him a look of hatred and disapproval, turns and departs, leaving Mrs. Lloyd looking completely dazed.

Mr. Lloyd Darling, are you all right?

Mrs. Lloyd But . . . this room is exactly the same as . . . that one . . .

In the corridor

Basil stands fuming.

In Alan's room

Polly is trying on one of Jean's dresses.

Polly Jean it's absolutely smashing.

Jean It's a bit tight over the bust.

Polly Oh I love it.

Alan Lower.

Jean (*to Polly*) Are you sure?

Polly So I'll pick it up tonight.

Alan Lower.

Alan Oh marvellous! That's it! Oooh!

In the corridor

Alan's voice Aaaaah! Beautiful! Oooh! Oh
baby, have you been taking lessons?

Polly's voice See you tonight.
Honestly, for £10 I think that's
fantastic!

Basil No, no, no, noooooooo . . .

Basil Polly, I want to see you at
reception in one minute in your hat
and coat.

Polly I'm sorry?

Basil I want to see you at reception in one minute in your hat and
coat.

Polly Will they fit you?

Basil Not . . . not . . . you! You know. You know.

He speeds into the inner office.

Basil They're going!

Sybil What?

Basil They're going!

*He races off again, back up the stairs, to
the Lloyd's room. He knocks abruptly,
and throws open the door.*

In the Lloyds' room

Basil I'm sorry, but you'll have to go. We made a mistake. These rooms are taken.

He looks round and finds the room empty.

Basil Hallo?

He turns and runs out of the room again, slamming the door behind him.

In Alan's room

Jean She was sitting on him!

Alan And then, five minutes later, I saw him lying on the floor underneath the waiter!

The door opens. Basil looks in and then stares at them.

Basil . . . Ah, there you are . . . . . . Yes, yes I might have guessed, mightn't I? Yes I see. Of course we're a bit behind the times down here in Torquay. Well. I'm afraid you'll have to go. Our mistake. I'm afraid these rooms are all taken. I'm sorry.

He goes. Then he comes back.

Basil Well actually, I'm not sorry. I mean, you come here, just like that, and well to be quite blunt, you have a good time at our expense. I mean, I think you know what I mean. Hah! You have had a <u>very</u> <u>very</u> good time haven't you? Well, not here you don't! Oh no. Thank you and goodnight!

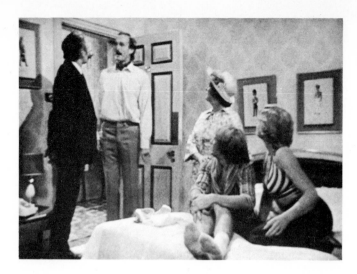

He slams the door and races off, leaving the occupants speechless.

In the office

Basil storms in.

Basil Well, that's taken care of that!

Sybil Basil, what is going on? Why did you tell Polly to get her hat and coat?

Basil Because she's going. Along with the Lloyds and that pair you let in. I've never seen anything like it in my life! <u>My</u> <u>God</u>!

Sybil Basil, what are you on about? Why are they going?

Basil I'll tell you why they're going. First of all, I go up there and I find that girl in his arms, in Lloyd's arms. Five minutes later he's got Polly in there!

Sybil What girl?

Basil That girl!

Sybil She's his daughter.

Basil What?

Sybil She's Mr. Lloyd's step-daughter. They're all one family.

Basil What about Polly then?

Sybil She was at school with Jean. They've known each other for years.

Basil For years, huh?

Sybil For years.

Basil . . . What have I done?

Sybil What have you done?

Basil I've told them to leave. Oh my God! What have I done?

Sybil You've told them to leave?

Basil Well, why didn't you tell me? How was I to know? Why didn't you tell me you <u>half-wit</u>? Why didn't they tell me?

Basil You can't blame me for this!

Sybil (*placidly*) Go and tell them they can stay.

Basil . . . Why don't you tell them?

Sybil I didn't tell them to go.

Basil No, no, I suppose it's all my fault, isn't it!

Sybil (*firmly*) Go and tell them! . . . Now!

Basil I won't.

Sybil You will.

Basil No, no I won't.

Sybil Oh yes you will.

Basil Oh yes I will. Right! Right! Leave it to me. Let me get you out of this. That's what I'm good for isn't it? Basil Fawlty Limited. Other people's messes cleared up. By appointment to my wife Sybil . . . . What am I going to say?

Sybil Tell them you made a mistake.

Basil Oh brilliant. Brilliant. Is that what made Britain great?

Basil 'I'm sorry I made a mistake'.

Basil What have you got for a brain, spongecake?

Sybil goes back to her work as Basil hurtles out.

In reception

Polly is approaching the desk in her hat and coat. Basil, hardly pausing on his way to the stairs, says . . .

Basil Er . . .very nice. Very nice.

Polly looks at him, quite dazed.

Basil Well, take it off, get back to work.

Basil sets off for the stairs, too preoccupied to notice Mr. Lloyd whom he passes at full-speed.

Basil (*to himself*) I'm so sorry I made a mistake.

Mr. Lloyd looks oddly after the disappearing Basil and starts to follow him.

In the upstairs corridor

Basil comes to top of the stairs, completely distracted, again addressing the void.

Basil I'm so sorry but I made a mistake.

Basil reaches Alan's room, knocks and opens the door.

In Alan's room

Basil comes in. All turn to look at him. He speaks very rapidly . . .

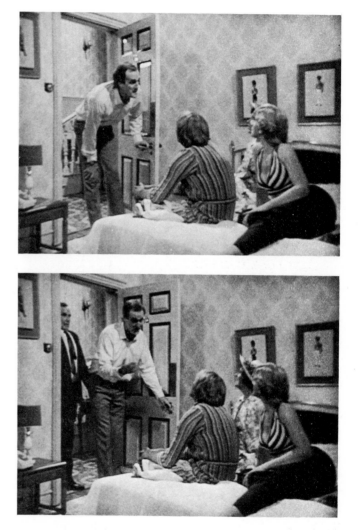

Basil I'm so sorry, but my wife has made a mistake.

Basil I don't know how she did it, but she did, she's made a complete pudding of the whole thing as usual, it'll be perfectly all right for you to stay, I've sorted it all out, I'm frightfully sorry but you know what women are like, they've only got one brain between the lot of them, well not all of them but some of them have, particularly my wife, so please do enjoy your stay and see you all later, thank you so much.

Basil spins round and sees Mr. Lloyd. He is in no mood for shocks. Quite demented he lets out a howl of surprise, doubles up for a moment with his hand on his heart, makes as if to hit Mr. Lloyd for a split second, pulls back, bows to him and says with great difficulty . . .

Basil . . . I was just saying . . . please do stay . . . they will explain . . . but my wife made a most dreadful mistake.

Basil retreats, bowing.

Mr. Lloyd Yes, I think she probably did.

The door closes.

In reception

Basil is at the desk. It is late and quite dark.
Major Gowen appears.

The Major Evening Fawlty

Basil Oh, evening Major.

The Major Papers arrived yet?

Basil Oh yes. Sorry it's so late. (*He hands one over*) Didn't get here till five, I'll have to have a word with them again.

The Major Where's your lady wife this evening?

Basil Oh she's spending the night at Audrey's. George has walked out on her again so she's in the usual state.

The Major Hmmm. Still I suppose it must have upset her a bit.

Basil Yes, but she makes such a song and dance about it.

The Major You don't care for Audrey, do you?

Basil Oh dreadful woman, dreadful.

The Major Still, very decent of your wife to go and listen to all that rubbish.

Basil Couldn't do without it Major.

The Major Fine woman, Mrs. Fawlty.

Basil No, no I wouldn't say that.

Major Nor would I. Well, goodnight Fawlty.

Basil Goodnight Major.

The Major goes upstairs. Basil finishes his work, turns the light off and his recorder on. It plays Chopin. Mrs. Peignoir comes in through the main doors.

Mrs. Peignoir Ah, Mr. Fawlty.

Basil Oh. Good evening. Sorry.

He turns off the recorder.

Mrs. Peignoir Oh don't turn it off. I love Chopin.

Basil Oh really? Hah. There's your key.

He switches it back on again.

Mrs. Peignoir Ah, it's so romantic!

Basil Exactly.

Mrs. Peignoir Mr. Fawlty, are you romantic?

Basil Good God no!

He switches off the tape.

Mrs. Peignoir Oh I think you are. Under that English exterior throbs a passion that makes Lord Byron look like a tobacconist.

Basil Oh, no. No way, as they say, ha ha.

Mrs. Peignoir Oh, don't look so bashful. I promise I won't try and sit on you again!

Basil Ah! Ha ha ha.

They begin to climb the stairs to the upstairs corridor.

Mrs. Peignoir And where is your charming wife this evening?

Basil Oh she's er . . . spending the night with a friend.

Mrs. Peignoir (*naughtily*) Oooh!

In the upstairs corridor

Basil A girl . . . lady friend.

Mrs. Peignoir Ah, while the cat's away . . .

Basil Oh hardly. There's so much to do. (*He glances at his watch*) Oh well, goodnight.

Mrs. Peignoir Goodnight . . . oh! Mr. Fawlty.

Basil . . . Yes?

Mrs. Peignoir Did you fix my window?

Basil Oh er . . . no . . . damn. Ha ha.

Mrs. Peignoir Would you mind? It's so hot tonight.

Basil Yes, yes. All right. OK.

They move off to Mrs. Peignoir's room.

In reception

In Mrs. Peignoir's room

Basil has lifted the sash window.

Basil Ah, there we are.

Mrs. Peignoir You're so strong.

Basil Well I'm sure you are too . . . if you put your mind to it. Well . . .

Mrs. Peignoir Your wife shouldn't leave you alone with strange women.

Basil Oh, I wouldn't call you that strange.

Mrs. Peignoir Oh Mr. Fawlty, you're so charming.

Basil Oh, only a little.

He looks hard at his watch.

Basil Good Lord!

Mrs. Peignoir Oh, feel that breeze, isn't it wonderful!

Basil (*backing out*) It is nice isn't it?

Mrs. Peignoir I shall sleep <u>au</u> <u>naturelle</u> tonight.

Basil Good idea!

Mrs. Peignoir Of course it's not so much fun on your own . . .

Basil Well, one can always pretend. Agh! Getting a twinge from the old leg, better go and lie down. Goodnight. Damned shrapnel.

Mrs. Peignoir Goodnight.

As Basil closes the door, he leaves Mrs. Peignoir giggling. He hurries down the corridor to his bedroom, closing the door with a sigh of relief.

In reception

Sybil switches off the light and makes for the stairs. But a loud bump comes alarmingly from the kitchen.

In the Fawltys' bedroom

Basil is pottering. There is a knock at the door.

Basil Hello, who is it?

Mrs. Peignoir's voice Oh, Mr. Fawlty.

Basil Oh.

He opens the door a fraction.

Basil Oh, hello.

Mrs. Peignoir I'm so sorry, I have to leave early tomorrow. Could I have a call at seven o'clock please?

Basil Oh, yes, wonderful, is that all, absolutely, seven it is, goodnight.

Mrs. Peignoir Please don't go yet.

Basil What? (*He looks at watch*) Oh <u>dear</u>.

Mrs. Peignoir I think you forgot something.

Basil Did I? Damn. Well, there you go. Goodnight.

Mrs. Peignoir Your recorder.

Basil . . . Oh.

Mrs. Peignoir You left it in my room.

Basil . . . Oh thank you.

Mrs. Peignoir You left it in my room so you could come and get it, didn't you?

Basil Ha ha ha!

Mrs. Peignoir I don't want you knocking on my door in the middle of the night.

Basil (*falsetto*) Ha ha ha ha ha . . . I should coco.

Mrs. Peignoir You naughty man! Goodnight.

Basil Goodnight.

He closes the door and locks it firmly.

In reception

Sybil is by the kitchen door listening to strange noises within. She hurries upstairs . . .

In the Fawltys' bedroom

The door handle turns. There is a knock. Basil sees the handle turning, squeals noiselessly and goes to the door making snoring noises. Sybil continues to knock, Basil to make his snores. He gives up and hisses . . .

Basil Oh God! Now go to your room. I won't ask you again.

In the corridor

Sybil Open the door.

In the Fawltys' bedroom

Basil No I can't. Listen, my wife just got back unexpectedly. She's in the bathroom.

Basil (*Loudly*) What dear? I think you'll find it on the second shelf Sybil darling.

Sybil Let me in!

Basil Look, you'll meet somebody else sooner or later.

She hammers on the door.

Basil Can't you control yourself! What sort of a place do you think this is? Paris?

Sybil's voice Let me in!!

Basil Shut up will you! Go away you great tart. Go <u>away</u>! My wife will hear us.

In the corridor

Sybil This <u>is</u> your wife.

In the bedroom

Realisation dawns. There are no first-class explanations. He opens the door.

Basil What a <u>terrible</u> dream.

But Sybil's mind is elsewhere.

Sybil There's a burglar downstairs.

Basil George got back did he?

Sybil There's a burglar downstairs. Quick!

Basil What?

Sybil A <u>burglar</u>!!

In reception

Basil is after a frying pan. He comes creeping down the stairs.

Basil Had enough?

Basil Manuel!!!!!?

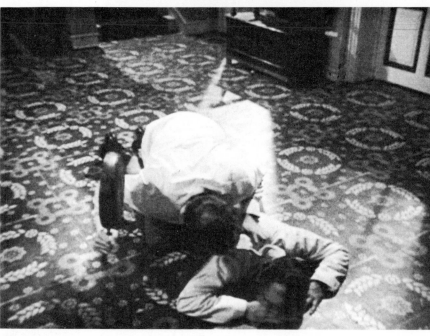

The lights go on.

Mr. Lloyd . . . . . . Goodnight.

They go upstairs.

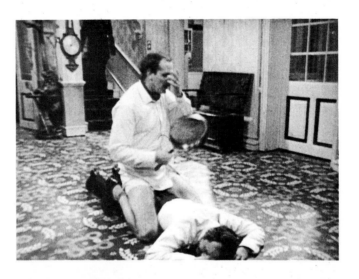

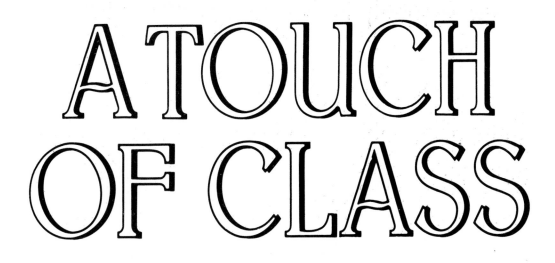

A TOUCH OF CLASS

CAST LIST

Basil Fawlty	**John Cleese**
Sybil Fawlty	**Prunella Scales**
Manuel	**Andrew Sachs**
Polly	**Connie Booth**
Major Gowen	**Ballard Berkeley**
Miss Tibbs	**Gilly Flower**
Miss Gatsby	**Renee Roberts**
Lord Melbury	**Michael Gwynn**
Danny Brown	**Robin Ellis**
Sir Richard Morris	**Martin Wyldeck**
Mr. Watson	**Lionel Wheeler**
Mr. Wareing	**Terence Conoley**
Mr. Mackenzie	**David Simeon**

In reception

Basil is on the phone.

Basil . . . One double room without bath for the 16th, 17th and 18th . . . yes, and if you'd be so good as to confirm by letter? . . . thank you so much, goodbye.

He puts the receiver down and takes a sip of tea. Sybil bustles in.

Sybil Have you made up the bill for room twelve Basil?

Basil I haven't yet, no.

Sybil Well they're in a hurry, Polly says they didn't get their alarm call.

She takes Basil's saucer and puts it away beneath the counter, leaving Basil a difficult manoeuvre to replace his cup.

Sybil And Basil, please get that picture up. It's been there for a week.

She returns to the office. Basil counts on his fingers.

Basil It's been there since Monday, Sybil . . . Tuesday . . . Wednesday . . . Thursday . . . (*to passing guests*) Good morning . . . Friday, Saturday . . .

He realises that Sybil is no longer there and snorts. He sees Manuel who is carrying three breakfast trays and goes across to him.

Basil Manuel! (*Slowly*) There is too much butter on those trays.

Manuel Que?

Basil There is too much butter, <u>on</u> <u>those</u> <u>trays</u>.

He points to each tray in turn.

Manuel No, no, no, Señor.

Basil What?

Manuel No, on . . . those . . . trays. No sir, uno dos tres. Uno . . . Dos . . . Tres

He points to each tray in turn.

Basil No, no. Hay mucho burro allí!

Manuel . . . Que?

Basil Hay . . . mucho . . . burro . . . allí!

Manuel Ah, mantequilla!

Basil What? Que?

Manuel points to the butter.

Manuel Mantequilla. Burro is . . . (*he brays like a donkey*).

Basil What?

Manuel Burro . . . (*he does more donkey imitations.*)

Basil Manuel, por favor, si, si . . .

Sybil has come back again.

Sybil What's the matter Basil?

Basil Nothing, I'm just dealing with it dear.

Manuel (*to Sybil*) He speak good . . . how you say . . . ?

Sybil English!

Basil Mantequilla . . . Solamante . . . dos . . . er . . .

Manuel . . . Dos?

Basil looks helplessly at Sybil.

Sybil Don't look at me. You're the one who's supposed to be able to speak it.

Basil angrily grabs all the spare butter from the trays.

Basil Two pieces! Two each! . . . Arriba, arriba!!

*He waves his hand towards the bedrooms
and Manuel runs off. Basil goes back
behind the desk, deposits the butter and
returns to the typewriter.*

Sybil I don't know why you wanted to hire him, Basil.

Basil Because he's cheap and keen to learn dear. And in this day
and age such . . .

Sybil But why did you say you could speak the language?

Basil (*grumpily*) I learnt classical
Spanish, not the strange dialect he
seems to have picked up . . .

Sybil It'd be quicker to train a monkey.

*Misses Tibbs and Gatsby come down the
stairs.*

Sybil (*with somewhat effusive charm*) Good morning Miss Gatsby,
morning Miss Tibbs.

Basil (*imitating the charm*) Good
morning, good morning.

Basil gets a look from Sybil. He hits a key
on the typewriter, gets the wrong one and
glares at it.

Sybil . . . Basil!

Basil Yes dear?

Sybil Are you going to hang the picture?

Basil Yes I am dear, yes, yes, yes.

Sybil When?

Basil When I've, when I've . . .

Sybil Why don't you do it now?

Basil Well I'm doing this dear . . .
I'm doing the menu.

Sybil You've got all morning to do the menu. Why don't you hang
the picture now?

Basil sighs heavily.

Sybil . . . Well?

He jumps up.

Basil Yes, yes, all right dear, yes, yes, I won't do the menu now . . .

He strides across the lobby saying
petulantly . . .

Basil I don't think you know how long it takes to do these menus
but no, it doesn't matter, I'll hang the picture now. If the menus are
late for lunch it doesn't matter, the guests can all come and look at
the picture till they are ready, right?

He starts to hang the picture, adjusting it
to his satisfaction.

Sybil . . . Lower.

Basil lowers it.

Sybil . . . Lower.

Basil grits his teeth, but lowers it again.

Sybil . . . Up a bit. There!

She disappears.

Basil Thank you dear. Thank you so much. I don't know where I'd
be without you . . . in the land of the living probably . . .

*He holds the picture in position. A young
couple, the Mackenzies, come hurridly
down the stairs and ring the bell.*

Basil . . . Yes?

Mr. Mackenzie Oh, could we have our bill please?

Basil Well can you <u>wait</u> a minute?

Mr. Mackenzie Er . . . I'm afraid we're a bit late for our train, we didn't get our alarm call.

Basil glowers at them, then he preremptorily puts the picture on the floor and strides back to the typewriter.

Basil Right. I was up at five you know, we do have staff problems, I'm so sorry it's not all done by magic . . .

Sybil looks in from the office.

Sybil Basil, are you doing the menu?

Basil No I'm not doing the menu dear. I am doing the bill for these charming people who are in a hurry.

Mr. Mackenzie (*to Sybil*) I'm sorry to cause all this trouble but the reason we're late is we didn't get our alarm call.

Sybil Oh dear I <u>am</u> sorry. (*Sweetly*) Basil, why didn't they get their alarm call?

Basil Because <u>I forgot</u>!

Basil I am so sorry I am not perfect!

He thrusts over the bill.

Basil There you are, there's the bill. Perhaps you'd pay my wife, I have to put the picture up . . . if there aren't any dustbins to be cleaned out . . .

He stalks towards the picture again. A newspaper boy comes in and puts his papers on the table.

Newspaper boy Newspapers!

Basil turns after him aggressively, tapping his watch. The boy exits rapidly. The Mackenzies leave the hotel, passing Basil who puts on his hospitable smile. It lacks integrity.

Basil Good-bye. See you again!

He collects the papers from the table – Sybil comes out to pick up a magazine.

Sybil Don't forget the picture Basil.

Basil I won't dear, leave it to me.

Sybil I'm going out now. I expect it to be up when I get back.

She leaves. Basil clenches his teeth.

Basil Drive carefully dear . . .

In the dining room

Basil comes in with the papers, goes straight to the Major, and gives him one of them. He ignores the other guests.

Basil Ah, good morning Major.

The Major Morning, Fawlty.

Basil I do apologise for the tardiness of the arrival of your newspaper this morning Major. I will speak to them again, see if something can be done.

The Major is looking at the headlines.

The Major Ah, more strikes . . . dustmen . . . post office . . .

Basil It makes you want to cry doesn't it? What's happened to the old ideal of doing something for your fellow man, of service? I mean today . . .

Another guest addresses Basil.

Mr. Watson Mr. Fawlty?

Basil Yes, I'm coming, I'm coming, wait a moment!

Basil (*To the Major, quietly*) They treat you like dirt you know . . . of course it's pure ignorance, but with the class of guest one gets nowadays . . .

The Major Ah! D'Olivera got a hundred!

Basil Did he? Did he really? Good for him, good old Dolly. Well, well, well . . .

Polly arrives with a cup of tea. Basil takes it, and gives her the other papers.

Basil Thank you Polly.

Mr. Watson (*apologetically*) We're only staying till Sunday!

Basil (*glaring*) Thank you.

He turns to the sideboard, helps himself liberally and makes his way through reception into the inside office . . .

In the office

Basil sits down. He hears Sybil coming, gives a start, and deftly pushes his snack out of sight.

Basil Ah, I thought you were going out dear.

Sybil is holding out a page of 'Country Life'.

Sybil What's this?

Basil I decided, Sybil, to advertise, I . . .

Sybil How much did it cost?

Basil . . . oh . . . I haven't . . . not a . . . fifteen?

Sybil Forty.

Basil (*vaguely*) . . . Forty . . .

Sybil I have told you where we advertise.

Basil Sybil, I know the hotel business.

Sybil No you don't, Basil.

Basil Sybil, we've got to try to attract a better class of person.

Sybil Why?

Basil Well, we're losing tone.

Sybil We're making money.

Basil Yes, yes . . .

Sybil Just.

Basil . . . But now we can try to build up a higher class of clientele! . . . Turn away some of the riff-raff.

Sybil So long as they pay their bills, Basil.

Basil Is that all that matters to you Sybil? Money??

Sybil This advertisement is a waste of forty pounds.

She turns to leave.

Basil One moment! One moment, please!

He picks up a letter from the desk and hands it to Sybil with a flourish.

Basil Well?

He waits triumphantly. Sybil glances at it,
quite unimpressed.

Sybil . . . Well?

Basil My dear woman, Sir Richard and Lady Morris, arriving this evening. For two nights. You see, they saw the advertisement in 'Country Life'.

Sybil I wish they were staying a week.

Basil Well so do I . . .

Sybil Might pay for the ad then.

She makes to leave again.

Basil Sybil, look! If we can attract this class of customer, I mean . . . the sky's the limit!

Sybil Basil, twenty-two rooms is the limit!

Basil I mean, have you, . . . <u>seen</u> the people in room six? They've never even sat on chairs before. They are the commonest, vulgarest, most horrible, nasty . . .

Sybil has gone. Basil shakes his head and sits wearily down to his toast. But before he can start the reception bell rings. He gets up with a deep sigh and, setting his face, walks back to reception.

In reception

Standing at the counter is a very non-aristocratic looking cockney, Danny Brown. He smiles.

Danny 'Allo!

Basil stands, appalled.

Danny Got a room?

Basil . . . I beg your pardon?

Danny Got a room for tonight, mate?

Basil . . . I shall have to see, sir . . . single?

Danny Yeah. No, make it a double, I feel lucky today!

At that moment Polly walks by to leave a newspaper on the desk. Danny looks at her appreciatively . . .

Danny 'Allo . . .

Polly (*smiling nicely*) Good morning.

Danny turns, following her round until she disappears. He looks at Basil who is staring at him with loathing.

Danny (*lightly*) Only joking!

Basil slams the register shut.

Basil No we haven't!

Danny What?

Sybil comes in, ready to sort things out . . .

Basil No, we haven't any rooms. Good day . . .

Sybil Number seven is free Basil.

Basil What? oh . . . Mr. Tone is in number seven dear.

Sybil No, he left while you were putting the picture up, Basil . . .
(*to Danny*) You have luggage sir.

Danny Just one case. (*To Basil, pointedly*). In the car . . . the white sports.

Basil closes his eyes in agony. Sybil rings the bell and asks Danny to register.

Sybil Fill this in would you sir?

Basil (*quietly*) If you can.

She glances at what Danny is writing.

Sybil I hope you enjoy your stay Mr. Brown.

Manuel arrives, and stands looking very eager.

Basil (*speaking slowly*) Er, Manuel would you take this gentleman's case from the car outside. Take it to room seven.

Manuel . . . Is not easy for me.

Basil What?

Manuel Is not easy for me . . . entender.

Basil Ah! Its not easy for you to understand. Manuel . . . (*to Danny*) we're training him . . . he is from Barcelona.

Basil In Spain.

Basil (*To Manuel*) Obtener la valisa . . .

Manuel Que?

Basil La valisa en el er, auto bianco sportiv . . . y . . . a la sala . . . siete . . . e . . . por favor.

Manuel Is impossible.

Basil What?

Manuel Is impossible.

Basil Look, it's quite simple!

Danny (*fluently*) Manuel, Sirvase buscar mi equipaje que esta en el couche blanco y lo traer a la sala numero siete.

Manuel Ah si senor. Habla Espanol!

Danny Sol un poco. Lo siento pero ha olbidau mucho.

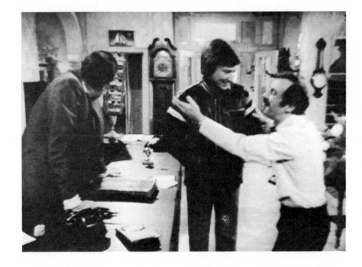

Manuel Non, no habla muy bien. Muy muy bien. Formidable!

Danny Gracias, gracias.

Manuel Lo voy a cojer ahora.

Manuel runs off to get the case. Basil looks hatefully at Danny.

Basil . . . . . Well, if there's anything else, I'm sure Manuel will be able to tell you . . . as you seem to get on so well together.

Basil goes into the office. Danny calls out . . .

Danny Key?

Basil re-enters, and takes the key from its hook.

He returns to the office.

In the office

Basil sits down at his desk, takes a deep breath, and switches on Brahms. He settles back in rapture.

In reception

Basil Hallo, dear . . . just doing the picture.

Sybil Don't forget the menu.

Basil . . . I beg your pardon?

Sybil Don't forget the menu.

Basil I thought you said you wanted . . . (*puts the picture down*) Right! I'll do the menu.

He almost throws the picture back on the floor and crosses abruptly to the reception desk.

Sybil You could have had them both done by now if you hadn't spent the whole morning skulking in there listening to that racket . . .

She walks towards the front door.

Basil Racket? That's <u>Brahms</u>! Brahms' Third Racket . . . (*to himself*) The whole morning!! I had two bars . . .

He hits the first key and gets it wrong again.

In the dining room

Polly has her pencil poised.

Polly Ready to order?

Danny Er, yeah. Whats a gralefrit?

Polly Grapefruit.

Danny And creme pot . . . pot rouge?

Polly Portuguese. Tomato soup.

Danny I'll have the gralefrit. Now, balm carousel . . . lamb?

Polly Casserole.

Danny Sounds good. Doesn't come with a smile?

Polly It comes with sprouts or carrots.

Danny Oh, smile's extra is it?

Polly You'll get one if you eat up all your sprouts.

Danny looks round and half registers a figure on the other side of the room.

Danny Waiter!

Basil freezes and then comes balefully towards Danny.

Basil . . . . . . I beg your pardon?

Danny . . . Oh 'allo. Can I have some wine please?

Basil The waiter is busy, sir, but I will fetch the carte des vins when I have finished attending to this gentleman.

Basil indicates the table he has just left.

Danny Oh fine. No hurry.

Basil returns, muttering . . .

Basil Oh good, how nice, how very thoughtful . . .

Back at the other table he asks . . .

Basil I trust the beer is to your satisfaction, sir?

Mr. Watson . . . . . . Yeh, fine.

Basil Ah good. May I wish you bon appetit.

Basil turns away, calling imperiously to Manuel and snapping his fingers.

Basil Manuel!

Manuel comes running into the dining room.

Basil Would you fetch the wine list please?

Manuel (*beaming uncomprehendingly*). Si senor.

Basil . . . The <u>wine</u> list. The wine . . . vino.

Manuel starts moving away towards the kitchen. Basil catches his arm.

Basil No no. The list. There, there, the list!

Basil points to it.

Basil The list, there! The red . . . <u>there</u>! . . . <u>there</u>!!

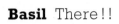

Basil There!!

Danny 'Ave you got a half bottle of the Beaujolais?

Basil Yes.

Danny Oh, fine.

Basil withdraws the wine list with a defiant flourish.

Danny's grapefruit lands on the floor.

    Basil Never mind! Never mind! Another grapefruit for table twelve please . . . Manuel!!

Polly dashes off as Manuel comes in. Basil points at the fallen grapefruit and turns to the other guests.

    Basil I'm so sorry. I do apologise . . .

Manuel picks up the grapefruit and cleans it. Basil starts to watch him. He is clearly going to replace it on the table.

Basil . . . No!! . . . Throw it away.

Manuel . . . Que?

Basil Throw . . . it . . . away!

Basil mimes a throw. Manuel is hesitant.

Basil Now!!!

Manuel throws the grapefruit away. Basil retrieves it, grabs Manuel and runs with him out of the room. He addresses the various tables as he passes . . .

Basil Sorry! . . . Sorry! . . . Sorry!

The two of them disappear. There is a yelp from Manuel. Polly appears bearing Danny's new grapefruit.

Polly Sorry about that.

Danny No, I like a bit of cabaret.

Danny picks up a sketch pad from his table.

Danny You left your sketch.

Polly Oh! Sorry.

She takes it.

Danny Its very good. Do you sell any?

Polly . . . Enough to keep me in waitressing.

She leaves as Basil reappears with the Beaujolais. He makes for the sideboard saying, rather pointlessly . . .

Basil One half bottle of beaujolais.

He is about to open the bottle when the reception bell rings.

Basil . . . Sybil!

Sybil pops her head round the door.

Sybil Someone at reception dear.

She vanishes.

Basil grits his teeth and steams through to greet the newcomer.

In reception

Basil hurries bad-temperedly into the lobby. A distinguished looking gentleman is standing there. He is called Melbury.

Basil Yes, yes, well yes?

The new visitor is slightly thrown by the force of this attack.

Melbury . . . Er, well, I was wondering if you could offer me accommodation for a few nights?

Basil (*very cross*) Have you booked?

Melbury . . . I'm sorry?

Basil Have you booked, have you booked?

Melbury No.

Basil (*to himself*) Oh dear!

He goes behind the desk.

Melbury . . . Why, are you full?

Basil Oh, we're not full . . . We're not <u>full</u> . . .

Basil Of course we're not <u>full</u>!!

Melbury I'd like er . . .

Basil (*rudely*) One moment, please.

Soon Basil is ready.

Basil . . . Yes?

Melbury A single room with a . . .

Basil Your <u>name</u> please, could I have your name?

Melbury Melbury.

The phone rings. Basil picks it up and gestures Melbury not to interrupt him.

Basil (*To Melbury*). One second please.

Basil (*To phone*) Hello? . . . Ah yes Mr.
O'Reilly, well, it's very simple really.
When I asked you to build me a wall
I was rather hoping that instead of
just dumping the bricks in a pile you
might have found time to cement them
together . . . you know, one on top
of the other in the traditional fashion.

Basil (*To Melbury, testily*). Could you fill it in please? (*To phone*) . . .
Oh splendid! When? Yes, I know Mr. O'Reilly but when?

Melbury is having difficulty with the register
Basil points a finger.

Basil (*To Melbury*) There, <u>there</u>! (*To phone*) Yes but when? Yes, yes,
aah! . . . the flu! (*To Melbury*) Both names please. (*To phone*) Yes, I
should have guessed, yes, flu and the Potato Famine no doubt . . .

Melbury I beg your pardon?

Basil Would you put <u>both</u> your names please . . . (*to phone*) Well
will you give me a <u>date</u>?

Melbury Er . . . I only use one.

Basil (*with a withering look*) You don't have a first name?

Melbury I am <u>Lord</u> Melbury, . . . so I sign myself Melbury.

There is a long, long pause.

Basil (*to phone*) . . . Go away.

Basil puts the phone down.

Basil . . . I'm <u>so</u> sorry to have kept you waiting, your lordship . . . <u>please</u> forgive me. Now, was there something, is there something, anything, I can do for you? Anything . . . at all?

Melbury Well, I have filled this in . . .

Basil Oh, don't bother with that please.

He takes the registration form and tosses it away.

Basil Now, a special room . . . a single? A double? A suite? Well we don't have any suites, but we have some beautiful doubles with a view . . .

Melbury No, no, just a single.

Basil Just a single! Absolutely! How very <u>wise</u> if I may say so, your honour.

Melbury With a bath.

Basil Naturally, naturally! <u>Naturellement</u>!

He roars with laughter.

    Melbury . . . I shall be staying for . . .

    Basil Oh please! Please! . . . Manuel!!

He bangs the bell. Nothing happens.

    Basil . . . Well, it's . . . it's rather grey today, isn't it?

    Melbury Oh yes, it is rather.

    Basil Usually its quite beautiful down here, but today is a real old . . .
er . . . rotter . . . Manuel!!!

Another bang on the bell.

    Basil Still . . . its good for the wheat.

Melbury Yes, er, I suppose so.

Basil Oh yes! I hear it's coming along wonderfully at the moment!
Thank God! Oh I love the wheat . . . there's no sight like a field of
wheat waving in the . . . waving in the . . . <u>Manuel</u>!!!

He bangs the bell as hard as he can.
No result.

Basil . . . Well how are you? I mean, if it's not a personal question. Well it is a personal . . .

He dashes from behind the desk.

Basil Let me get your cases for you, please allow me . . .

Melbury . . . Oh, thank you, they're just outside.

Basil Splendid. Thank you so much. I won't be one moment . . .

Basil sprints off, collects the cases and returns to find Sybil talking to Lord Melbury at the counter.

Basil . . . Ah, Lord Melbury. May I introduce my wife?

Melbury Yes, we have met.

Basil Oh good.

Sybil Thank you, Basil.

Basil My wife, may I introduce Your Lordship.

Sybil Basil, we've sorted it out.

Basil Splendid, splendid.

Melbury I wonder, could I deposit this case with you . . . just a few valuables . . .?

Basil takes it at once.

Basil Valuables, of course. Please let me take it now. I'll put it in the safe straight away.

Basil Sybil, would you put this in the safe please?

Sybil I'm just off to the kitchens, Basil.

Basil (*muttering angrily*) Yes, well if you're busy . . .

Sybil Nice to have met you Lord Melbury. I hope you enjoy your stay.

Sybil leaves.

Basil Yes well I'll do it then, then I'll do the picture . . . (*change of mood*) I'll put this away in one moment, your Lord.

Manuel has appeared at last.

Basil Manuel, will you take these cases to room twenty-one.

Manuel . . . Que?

Basil Take . . . to room . . . twenty-one.

He surreptitiously signals the number with his fingers. Manuel watches them bemused.

Manuel . . . No entender.

Basil Prenda las casos en . . . oh doesn't matter. Right! I'll do it, I'll do it. Thank you, Manuel.

He flies round the desk to the cases. Manuel tries to be helpful . . .

Manuel . . . I take them.

Basil No, no, go away!

Manuel Que?

They struggle across the hall together.

Basil Go and wait!

Manuel Wait?

Basil nods in the direction of the dining room.

Basil In there! Go and wait in <u>there</u>! Go and be a waiter in there, ha! ha! ha!

Manuel runs off into the dining room. Basil turns back to Lord Melbury.

Basil I <u>do</u> apologise, your lordship, I'm afraid he's only just joined us, we're training him. It'd be quicker to train a monkey. Ha ha ha!

Basil's laugh freezes as Lord Melbury stands motionless. Then he goes quickly upstairs with the cases. A pause. He returns into view.

Basil Do please follow me . . . I mean, if you're ready. There's no hurry . . .

Melbury Oh, yes, fine.

Melbury follows Basil upstairs.

In the dining room

There is peace as people eat and talk quietly. Then Basil hurries in and makes straight for a table by the window where Mr. and Mrs. Wareing and their son are sitting placidly. He removes a wine bottle from Mr. Wareing's grasp and puts it down firmly.

Basil Excuse me, I'm so sorry to bother you. Would you mind moving to that table?

Mr. Wareing . . . What?

Basil Could I ask you to move to that table over there?

Mr. Wareing But . . .

Basil I'm so sorry to trouble you.

Mr. Wareing gets to his feet, protesting.

Mr. Wareing We're halfway through . . .

Basil Thank you so much.

Mr. Wareing Yes, but . . .

Basil This is Lord Melbury's table you see.

Mr. Wareing What?

Basil Lord Melbury. When he stays with us he always sits at this table.

Mr. Wareing Well why did they put us here?

Basil Ah, an oversight . . . on my wife's part. He's just arrived you see. Would you mind? Polly! Would you help these people to that table? Thank you, thank you so much.

The family get up very unwillingly. Polly, slightly puzzled, starts moving the dishes. Mrs. Wareing is particularly slow . . .

Basil Come on! <u>Come on</u>!! . . . Thank you.

They all go. Basil takes a vase of flowers from somebody else's table and puts it down on Lord Melbury's table-to-be. Lord Melbury comes in. Basil turns to him ingratiatingly.

Basil Ah, Lord Melbury! Do please come this way . . . Your Lordship . . .

Basil I have your table over here by the window . . . as usual.

Melbury glances at Basil who gives him a slight wink. Melbury doesn't understand.

Basil Just here . . . thank you so much.

Melbury Thank you, thank you very much . . .

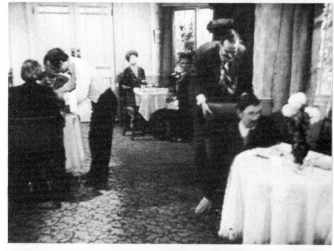

Basil I'm <u>so</u> sorry. Oh my Lord!
Oh my God!!

Wareing I think he's killed him!

Basil Get on with your meals!!!
Thank you so much.

He starts trying to do what he can to make amends.

In reception

Basil is doing the pools. He looks up sharply as he hears the dining room door open. Lord Melbury emerges wiping himself down with a handkerchief. Basil is with him in an instant.

Basil Lord Melbury. I really must apologise again for . . .

Melbury Please, please, think nothing of it.

Basil But it was so . . .

Melbury Please! It was the smallest of accidents, it could have occurred anywhere.

Basil Yes but . . .

Melbury No, no, no, I've forgotten all about it.

Basil That's most . . . you're really . . . er, your Lordship, would you allow me to offer you dinner here tonight . . . as our guest?

Melbury That's extremely kind of you. Unfortunately I have an engagement tonight . . .

Basil (*mortified*) Oh!

Lord Melbury suddenly thinks of something.

Melbury Oh, actually . . .

Basil Yes! Yes!!

Melbury There is one thing.

Basil Good! Good!

He goes eagerly back behind the desk.

Melbury I was wondering . . . could you cash me a small cheque? I'm playing golf this afternoon.

Basil Oh, delighted!

Melbury And I'd rather not go into the town . . .

Basil Absolutely . . . I mean, er how much? . . . er, if it's not a rude question.

Melbury Er well . . . er . . . could you manage . . . fif . . .

He looks inside his wallet.

Melbury Oh! . . . a hundred?

Basil A . . . h . . . hundred? (*He recovers and gushes*) Oh
absolutely . . . Oh yes, I mean will a hundred be enough? . . . I mean
a hundred and fifty . . . two . . . two . . . er, a hundred and sixty?

Lord Melbury reflects.

Melbury . . . Let's see, that's, er,
dinner tonight . . . few tips . . . of
course it's the weekend isn't it . . .
is two hundred all right?

Basil (*momentarily shattered*) Oh. (*Then an extravagant gesture*)
Oh! <u>Please</u>! Yes! Oh, ha ha! oh tremendous! Oh. . . I'm so happy!
I'll send someone to the town straightaway and have it for you when
you get back.

Melbury Yes well that would be splendid . . . thank you.

Basil Oh, not at all, my
privilege . . .

*Lord Melbury exits, leaving Basil in a
transport of delight.*

Basil . . . What breeding . . . sheer
. . . ooh!

*He starts to write out the cheque. Sybil
walks in. In a flash Basil whips the cheque
book behind his back and gives her a peck
on the cheek.*

Basil Hallo dear.

Sybil What are you doing?

Basil I'm kissing you dear.

Sybil Well don't.

*Basil walks out from behind the desk
muttering . . .*

Basil Just thought it might be nice to . . .

Sybil I heard about lunch.

Basil What? . . . Oh that! Oh, think nothing of it.

Sybil What?

Basil It was the smallest of accidents. Could have occurred
anywhere.

Sybil Anywhere? First of all you move that nice family in the middle of their meal and then you attack Lord Melbury with a chair!

Basil walks back to the desk. He speaks pompously . . .

Basil Look Sybil, I've had a word with Lord Melbury about it. He was quite charming . . . Oh, it's delightful to have people like that staying here . . . sheer class, baths, engagements, golf, a couple of hund . . . h, h, horses . . .

Sybil Well, I've never seen such tatty cases.

Basil (*exasperated*) Of <u>course</u> you haven't. It's only the true upper class that would have tat like that . . . It's the whole point! . . . Oh, you don't know what I'm talking about . . .

He comes behind the counter.

Sybil No I don't. But don't ever move guests in the middle of a meal again . . . and get that picture up!

She departs into the office.

Basil . . . Sour old rat.

Polly comes into the lobby. Basil summons her, gets out his cheque book and speaks conspiratorially . . .

Basil . . . Ah! . . . Would you do me a favour? When you're down in town this afternoon . . . just between ourselves, don't mention it to my wife . . . pop into the bank and just . . .

In the town

Polly leaves the bank, crosses the street, and walks past a parked car, she checks, looks into it, and is surprised to see Danny Brown sitting in it with another man. Danny sees her, motions her urgently to get into it and she does so. He shows her an official looking card and points to a jewellers shop. At that moment Lord Melbury, comes out of the shop, looks round furtively, and hurries down the street. Danny nods in the direction of a waiting colleague who goes immediately in Melbury's direction. Danny and Polly watch . . .

In reception

Basil is holding the picture against the wall, marking the position with a pencil. The phone rings. Basil looks round at it.

Basil . . . Could someone answer that please?

Phone goes on ringing.

Basil . . . Hallo! Is there nobody who can answer that? There must be <u>someone</u> . . .

Manuel runs in and heads for the phone.

Basil Not you.

Manuel goes away. Basil puts the picture down and makes for the desk.

Basil . . . I'll never get it up. I'll cancel my holiday . . . get it done then.

He picks up the phone.

Basil Hello, Fawlty Towers . . .

The ringing continues. Sybil comes in and answers the other phone.

Sybil Hello, Fawlty Towers . . .

Basil lowers his receiver and glares at her.

Sybil Oh, hello Brenda . . . (*to Basil*) Basil, its six o'clock.

Basil puts down his receiver wearily as Sybil continues her conversation. Polly comes in and Basil goes over to her.

Basil (*whispers*) Ah,. Polly . . . Did you cash it?

Polly Yes, er . . . Mr. Fawlty . . .

Basil Good, good.

Polly (*urgently*) Could I have a word with you?

She hands him the money in an envelope.

Basil What?

Polly Could I speak to you in the office for just a minute . . . (*indicating the office*).

Basil Not <u>now</u> Polly!

Polly It's very important, I . . .

Basil Later! Later!

Sybil looks up from the phone.

Sybil Basil!

Basil I'm just going dear. Thank you Polly.

He runs off.

In the bar

Basil dashes behind the counter. He hears someone come in. As it is exactly six o'clock he doesn't need to see who it is.

Basil Ah, good evening Major.

The Major Evening Fawlty.

Basil The usual?

The Major looks at his watch.

The Major Er . . . er . . . oh, why not indeed?

He settles himself down.

The Major I've just been watching one of those nature films on television.

Basil Oh yes?

The Major Did you know that a female gibbon gestates for seven months?

Basil Seven months? Well I never . . .

The Wareing family come in. Mr. Wareing goes to the bar.

    Basil Ah, good evening Mr. Wareing.

    Mr. Wareing (*coldly*) A gin and orange, a lemon squash and a scotch and water please.

    Basil Certainly.

He starts to move away.

    Mr. Wareing . . . Is there any part of the room you'd like us to keep away from?

    Basil What? . . . (*false jollity*) Oh, ha ha ha.

    Mr. Wareing (*curtly*) We'll be over there then.

    Basil (*to the Major*) Seven! Well, well . . .

Lord Melbury enters the bar.

    Melbury Evening Fawlty.

Basil turns effusively.

Basil Ah good evening Lord Melbury.

Mr. Wareing, from a distance, makes his point again.

Mr. Wareing Anywhere?

Basil Yes anywhere, anywhere . . .
Your Lordship, may I offer you a little
aperitif . . . as our guest?

Melbury That's very kind of you . . .
dry sherry if you please.

Melbury wanders off.

Basil (*to the Major*) . . . What else?

Basil Such . . . oh, I don't know what . . .

The Major Je ne sais quoi?

Basil Exactly!

Sybil enters.

Basil Ah, there you are Sybil.

He departs Lord-wards with the dry sherry.

Sybil Good evening Major.

The Major Good evening Mrs. Fawlty.

Melbury is glancing at some coins in a display case. Basil brings him his drink.

Basil There you are your Lordship.

Melbury Ah, thank you very much.

Basil I see my little collection of coins tickles your interest.

Melbury What? Oh yes, yes.

Basil All British Empire of course. Used to be quite a hobby of mine . . . little investment too . . .

Melbury Quite . . . oh . . . talking of, er, did you manage to . . .

Basil Oh yes. Here you are your Lordship.

Back in the Bar

Melbury . . . Oh yes you know, these sorts of things, their value's soared in the last couple of years.

Basil Have they really?

Melbury Yes, yes. Take my advice. Get them revalued, and insure them for the full amount.

Basil Yes, yes, I will.

Melbury finishes his sherry and puts the glass on Basil's tray.

Melbury Can't take risks nowadays I'm afraid.

Basil No, no quite.

Melbury Well, I must be off.

He walks away, Basil obsequious in his wake.

Basil Thank you, thank you, your lord . . . I'll certainly . . .

Melbury Good-bye.

As Melbury leaves Sybil calls to Basil.

Sybil Basil!

Basil Yes, yes, I was just talking to Lord Melbury dear· . . .

Mr. Wareing A gin and orange, a lemon squash and a scotch and water please!

Basil I do apologise, I was just talking to Lord . . .

Melbury returns.

Melbury Fawlty!

Basil leaves the Wareings in mid-sentence.

Basil Yes Lord Melbury?

Basil backs across the room as Melbury advances, all awe and attention.

Melbury . . . I was just thinking . . . I'm having dinner tonight with the Duke of Buckleigh . . . do you know him?

Basil Not . . . . . . personally, no.

Melbury Oh . . . well, he's a great expert, you know, Sotheby's and all that . . .

Basil Is he?

Melbury Well if you liked, I could take them over with me, ask him to have a quick look at them . . . find out their current value.

Basil (*overwhelmed*) Would . . . would you really?

Melbury Yes, yes, certainly. Well, I'll be off in a few moments.

He leaves. Basil fawns after him.

Basil Well that's really . . . so incredibly . . . er . . .

Sybil Basil!!

Basil I'm talking to Lord Melbury!

Mr. Wareing (*slow and loud*) A . . . gin . . . and orange . . . a lemon squash . . . a scotch and water <u>please</u>!

357

Basil All right! All right!

The reception bell rings urgently.

In reception

It is Polly. Basil runs out clutching the coins in a box.

Polly Oh, Mr. Fawlty . . .

Basil Was that Lord Melbury? Has he gone?

Polly I rang Mr. Fawlty, I must speak with you.

Basil (*spluttering*) What? . . . can't you see I'm <u>busy</u>?

Polly Please! It's very important, can we talk in there?

She indicates the office.

Basil I can't!

Sybil calls from the bar.

Sybil's voice Basil!!

Basil (*shouting*) I'm just dealing with something important out here Sybil, thank you. (*To Polly*) All <u>right</u>!

He hurries into the office, followed by Polly.

In the office

Basil Yes? Yes, right, well, yes, yes, what is it?

Polly It's about Lord Melbury.

Basil Yes?

Polly He's not Lord Melbury . . . He's a confidence trickster.

Basil . . . I beg your pardon?

Polly Mr. Brown told me.

Basil Haaaa!

Polly Mr. Brown's from the CID. They've been watching Melbury because he's pulling some con trick at a jeweller's in the town. They're going to arrest him when he leaves the hotel so as not to cause you embarrassment. But he asked me to tell you . . .

Basil doesn't believe a word of it.

Basil Oh how nice of him!

Polly Please Mr. Fawlty . . .

Basil Of course, I don't know what other tales Mr. Brown of MI5 has been impressing you with but . . .

Polly He's a con man!

Basil Oh of course. It stands out a mile doesn't it? He's so <u>common</u>.

Basil Unlike that cockney git whose ulterior motive will soon no doubt become apparent to you, poor innocent misguided child that you are.

Enter Sybil, very businesslike.

Sybil Basil, what is going on?

Basil Nothing my dear, nothing at all.

Polly Mrs. Fawlty . . .

Basil Now look!

Sybil Yes Polly?

Basil I don't know what she's . . .

Sybil Basil!!!

Polly Mr. Brown's from the CID.

Basil Hah!

Polly He showed me his identification. They're watching Melbury. He's a confidence trickster.

Sybil . . . I see.

She goes straight to the safe.

Basil What . , . what do you mean, you see?

Sybil Let's have a look at these valuables. . . .

Basil Sybil, I forbid you to open that safe!

Basil Sybil, I forbid you to take out that case!

Basil Sybil, do not open that case! I forbid it.

Basil goes and sits down in dismay.

Basil . . . I never thought I would live to see the day when a . . . peer of the realm . . . entrusts to us . . . a case of valuables . . . in trust . . .

Sybil places the open case in front of him.
He looks into it for a long time.

Basil emits a strange growl.

Sybil I'll call the police.

Polly They're already here, Mr. Brown's outside.

Polly leaves. The reception bell rings.

Sybil Someone at reception, Basil.

Basil rises slowly and makes his way to the door. He clenches his fist in readiness . . .

In reception

But it is Sir Richard and Lady Morris, and not Lord Melbury, that he finds there. He adjusts slowly, his thoughts elsewhere.

Basil . . . Ah! . . . all right . . . er . . .

He smiles, pauses, and then collects himself.

Basil (*brightly*) Good evening.

Sir Richard I believe you were expecting us.

Basil No, I was expecting somebody else . . .

He goes into another reverie.

Sir Richard Sir Richard and Lady Morris.

Basil (*absently*) Yes, yes, them as well.

Sir Richard I'm sorry?

Basil How did you know?

Sir Richard What?

Basil Oh . . . <u>you're</u> Sir Richard and Lady Morris, I do beg your pardon. I was just think . . . er . . .

He goes off again, thinking revenge. He comes to . . .

Basil Now, would you mind filling this out, please, we've given you room . . .

Lord Melbury comes downstairs.

Basil . . . Ah hah!

Lord Melbury Ah Fawlty!

Basil Mr. Fawlty to you, Lord Melbury.

Lord Melbury I beg your pardon?

Basil Oh, nothing, please, forget all about it.

Lord Melbury Oh . . . er . . . well . . . here's the cheque for two hundred pounds . . .

Basil Ah, thank you so much.

The Morrises are transfixed.

Basil Now, about my priceless collection of coins . . .

Lord Melbury Oh yes . . . er do you still want . . .

Basil Do I still want you to take them to be valued by the Duke of Buckleigh, my lord?

Lord Melbury Er . . . yes.

Basil No, I don't. Because we've just heard, that the Duke of Buckleigh is . . . dead! Yes, he got his head knocked off by a golf ball. Tragic! Tragic!

A pause. Basil beams at Melbury.

Basil Well, how are you then Lord Melbury?

Basil 'Ow are yer then, mate?

Basil 'Ow's me old mucker!

Basil Any valuables to deposit Sir Richard . . . any bricks?

*Basil smiles at the Morrises. Sybil has
come beside him looking anxious . . .*

    Basil I do apologise . . .

    Basil You bastard!! . . .

    Basil (*courteous again*) We've given
you room twelve with the view
overlooking the park . . .

The police are in the building.

Basil Hello Lord Melbury!

Basil . . . <u>BASTARD</u>!!!!

People run in all directions.

Basil (*to the Morrises*) Please think
nothing of it.

*Manuel comes out of the dining room with
a chair. Melbury falls over it and is pinned
by a plain-clothes policeman. Basil walks across
smiling politely.*

Basil Do please excuse me one
moment.

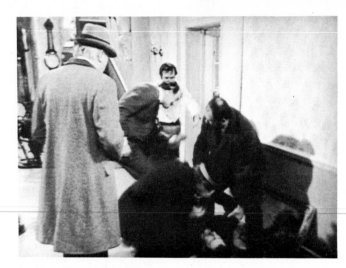

*Having put the boot in, he bends over the
body. He emerges with the envelope
and extracts his two hundred pounds.*

Sybil Basil, the Morrises are leaving.

Outside the hotel

The Morrises are getting into their car.
Basil hurtles down the steps.

Basil . . . Where are you going? . . . Where are you going . . . ?

Sir Richard We're leaving!

Basil Oh please don't. You'll like it here.

Sir Richard I've never been in such a place in my life.

Basil . . . You snob! You stupid . . .
stuck-up . . . toffee-nosed . . .
half-witted . . . upper class piles of
. . . pus!!

*Basil walks slowly and disconsolately back
up the steps. As he reaches the top he
sees Melbury being escorted out of the
hotel by three policemen.*

Basil (*imploringly*) Just one! Just one!

Policeman Sorry Mr. Fawlty.

Basil Oh just one, please.

But the policeman continues to restrain Basil. Basil gives up and steps backwards into a tub of flowers.

In the lobby

Basil enters.

Basil Well, I'd better put the picture up.

Basil pauses.

Basil Oh . . . thank you Polly for the, er . . . (*to Manuel*) Well done Manuel.

Manuel Que?

Basil Oh . . . . . . Olé.

Danny comes back in.

Danny I'm sorry about that Mr. Fawlty . . . can I buy you a drink?

Basil No, no, I'd better get this thing up I suppose . . .

Sybil enters with Mr. Wareing.

Sybil Basil!

Mr. Wareing (*very loudly*) A gin and orange . . . a lemon squash, . . . and a scotch and water <u>please</u>!!

Basil Right!

Basil Come on then . . .

THE GERMANS

CAST LIST

Basil Fawlty .... John Cleese

Sybil Fawlty .... Prunella Scales

Manuel .... Andrew Sachs

Polly .... Connie Booth

Major Gowen .... Ballard Berkeley

Sister .... Brenda Cowling

Doctor .... Louis Mahoney

Miss Tibbs .... Gilly Flower

Miss Gatsby .... Renee Roberts

Mr. Sharp .... John Lawrence

Mrs. Sharp .... Iris Fry

Large Woman .... Claire Davenport

First German .... Nick Kane

Second German .... Willy Bowman

In the hospital

It is a private ward. Sybil is eating chocolates.

Basil . . . So . . . you're sure you'll be all right?

Sybil . . . What, Basil?

Basil I said, you're sure you'll be all right?

Sybil Will you get me my bed jacket?

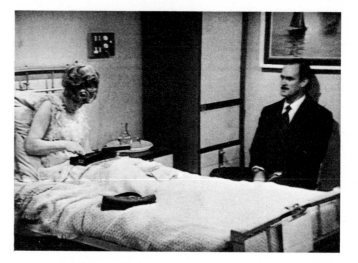

Basil Er . . . bed jacket.

Basil gets up and fumbles in the drawer beside the bed. It is the wrong chest of drawers.

Sybil In the drawer, the blue one. In the <u>drawer</u>.

Basil crosses the room, sighing a little. More fumbling.

Sybil Now you won't forget the fire drill tomorrow, will you?

Basil No, I won't dear, no, I can cope you know . . . This one?

It is pink.

Sybil That's not blue.

Basil (*unwilling to concede*) . . . It's got blue things on it.

Sybil (*placidly*) They're flowers, and I didn't ask you for the one with the flowers, did I?

Basil No you didn't. Quite right. I only picked that one up to annoy you actually. I mean, what have you got all this stuff <u>for</u>?

Sybil What?

Basil You're only here for three days. Are you going to play charades every night? . . . This one?

Sybil Is it blue?

It is bright blue.

Basil . . . It's bluish, I suppose.

Sybil Now you will remember to collect the stuff from Thomas's won't you?

Basil Yes, I will.

Sybil Oh, and I forgot to scrape the mould off the cheddar this morning, so remind Chef.

Basil Right.

Sybil And <u>do</u> try and find time to put the moose's head up.

Basil Oh.

Sybil It's been sitting there for <u>two</u> <u>weeks</u>, Basil.

Basil Yes, yes, yes.

Sybil I don't know why you bought it.

Basil It'll lend the lobby a certain <u>ambience</u> Sybil. It has a touch of <u>style</u> about it.

Sybil It's got a touch of mange about it.

Basil That is not so.

Sybil It's got things living in it Basil . . . It's nasty.

Basil It is not nasty. It is superb.

Sybil I'm not going to argue with you Basil, just get it up out of the way. I don't want to snag any more cardies on it. And will you give me my telephone book please?

*Basil gets up and prowls about looking
for the telephone book.*

Basil It's not as though I don't have enough to do you know. I'm on my own, we've got the Germans arriving tomorrow . . .

Sybil Not till lunchtime. You could do it in the morning.

Basil I've got the fire drill in the morning!

Sybil That only takes ten minutes . . . In the bag.

*Basil now peers around for a bag, saying
only half to himself.*

Basil I thought slavery'd been abolished.

Sybil Don't you ever think of anyone but yourself?

Basil Oh.

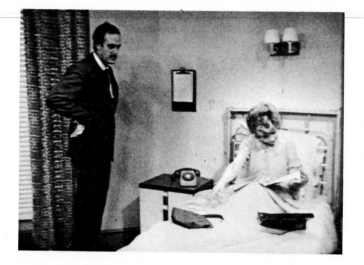

Sybil In the bag.

She points it out to him.

Basil Oh yes, in the bag. You let me do it. (*He rummages inside*) You just lie there with your feet up and I'll go and carry you up another hundredweight of lime creams . . .

He finds the book and hands it over.

Sybil I'm actually about to have an operation Basil.

Basil Oh yes, how is the old toe-nail? Still growing in, hmmm? (*He sits on the bed*) Still burrowing its way down into the bone? Macheting its way through the nerve, eh? Nasty old nail.

Sybil It's still hurting, if that's what you mean Basil.

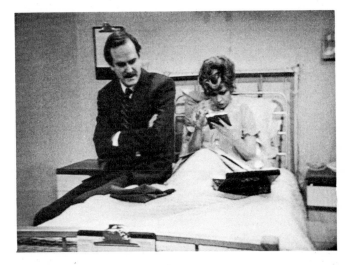

Basil Well it'll be out in the morning, poor little devil. I wonder if they'd mount it for me just for old time's sake?

Sybil I'm sure it's worth asking. You could hang it on the wall next to the moose. They'd go rather well together.

Basil Ha, ha, ha.

At this moment the sister enters briskly . . .

Sister (*to Sybil*) Ah, there we are. (*To Basil*) Come on, out you go.

She starts bustling round. Basil peers under the bed and gets to his feet.

Basil Oh, were you talking to me? I'm sorry, I thought there was a dog in here.

Sister Oh no, no dogs in here.

Basil (*looking at her closely*) I wouldn't bet on it.

Sister Oh no, not allowed. Now come along, you're in the way.

She busies herself round Sybil.

Basil . . . Fawlty's the name. <u>Mr</u>. Fawlty.

Sister Let's sit you up a bit now.

Sybil (*very sweetly*) Thank you sister.

*Basil has sat down. Sister gives Sybil
a thermometer.*

Sister Just pop that under your tongue.

She sees Basil.

Sister . . . You still here?

Basil . . . Apparently.

Sister (*by way of explanation*) The doctor's coming.

Basil jumps up, startled.

Basil My God! A doctor, here, in the hospital? Whatever can we do?

Sister You can leave!

Basil (*reflectively*) Why do they call you 'Sister'? Is it a term of endearment?

Sybil makes a warning noise. She wants to speak but the thermometer prevents her.

Sister Now look Mr. Fawlty, I'm not going to ask you again.

Basil Presumably you wouldn't mind if I said good-bye to my wife? She is under the knife tomorrow.

Sister It's only an ingrowing toe-nail!

Basil Oh you know do you? That'll be a help.

He bends down to Sybil.

Basil Well goodbye dear. Take care. And if you can think up any more things for me to do, don't hesitate to call.

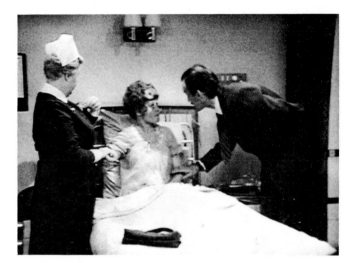

Another loud noise from Sybil.

Sister . . . Finished?

Basil Just, yes. Thank you so much.

Sister Not at all.

Basil Charmed I'm sure.

He starts to leave, but turns back to sister.

Basil Ingrowing toe-nail. Right foot. You'll find it on the end of the leg.

Outside Sybil's ward

He sweeps out of the room, almost colliding with a doctor who is just about to come in.

Doctor Mr. Fawlty?

Basil Yes?

Doctor Doctor Fin.

Basil Oh, how do you do doctor?

Doctor You've just seen your wife?

Basil Yes. Just said good-bye . . .well, au revoir.

Doctor Yes, well, it's a very simple operation. But it'll be quite painful afterwards.

Basil Will it, will it, oh dear.

Doctor Just for a time, but please don't worry.

Basil Right. Well, no I'll try not to . . . Quite painful?

Doctor Yes.

The doctor goes into the ward.

In reception

Basil struts in and goes towards the desk.
Major Gowen is in the lobby.

Basil (*breezily*) Evening Major.

The Major Oh, evening Fawlty.
Hampshire won.

Basil Did it? Oh isn't that good, how splendid!

The Major Oh Fawlty, how's . . . um . . . um . . .

Basil . . . My wife?

The Major . . . That's it, that's it.

Basil Fine, absolutely fine. They're taking it out tomorrow morning.

The Major Is she? oh good.

Basil Not her, the nail. They won't have operated till tomorrow.

The Major What?

Basil The nail. They're taking it out tomorrow.

The Major . . . How did she get a nail in her?

Basil I thought I told you Major, she's having her toe-nail out.

The Major What, just one of them?

Basil Well, it's an ingrowing one Major.

The Major Ah well . . . if it's causing you pain . . . you have it out.

Basil Exactly. So . . . I'm on my own now, start running this place properly.

The Major . . . So you're on your own now are you?

Basil . . . Apparently.

The Major Still, she won't be gone for long will she?

Basil No, no, no, not unless there's a serious mistake.

The Major Still . . . you've always got Elsie to help you.

Basil . . . Who?

The Major Elsie.

Basil Well she . . . er she left a couple of years ago Major.

The Major Funny . . . I thought I saw her yesterday.

Basil I don't think so. She's in Canada.

The Major . . . Strange creatures, women.

Basil Well, we can't stand about here all day . . .

*But the Major is in full conversational
spate . . .*

The Major I knew one once . . . striking looking girl . . . tall, you
know . . . father was a banker.

Basil Really.

The Major Don't remember the name of the bank.

Basil Never mind.

The Major . . . I must have been rather keen, because I took her to
see India.

Basil India?

The Major At the Oval . . .

The Major Fine match, marvellous finish . . . Surrey had to get thirty-three in about half an hour . . . she went off to powder her . . . hands or something . . . never came back.

Basil What a shame.

The Major But the strange thing was . . . throughout the morning she kept referring to the Indians as niggers. 'No no,' I said, 'the niggers are the West Indians. These people are wogs.' 'No,' she said, 'All cricketers are niggers.'

Basil They do get awfully confused don't they? They're not thinkers. I see it with Sybil every day.

The Major . . . I do wish I could remember her name. She's still got my wallet.

Basil As I was saying, no capacity for logical thought.

The Major Who?

Basil Women.

The Major Oh yes, yes, . . . I thought you meant Indians.

Basil No, no, no, no . . . Wasn't it Oscar Wilde who said 'They have minds like Swiss cheese'?

The Major What do you mean . . . hard?

Basil No no, full of holes.

The Major Really? Indians?

Basil No, <u>women</u>!

The Major Oh.

Polly comes into reception and bends down behind Basil looking for something.

Basil Yes, can we help you?

Polly Hello.

Basil You see. Three years at college and she doesn't know the time of day.

The Major It's . . . er . . . just two minutes to six.

Basil (*to Polly*) What are you looking for?

Polly My German book.

Basil (*to the Major*) We've got some Germans arriving tomorrow Major, so Polly's brushing up another one of her languages.

The Major Germans! Coming here?

Basil Just for a couple of days Major.

The Major . . . I don't care much for Germans . . .

Basil I know what you mean but . . .

The Major Bunch of Krauts, that's what they are, all of 'em. Bad eggs!

Basil Yes, well forgive and forget Major . . . God knows how, the bastards. Still, I'd better get the moose up.

The Major You've got to love 'em though, haven't you?

Basil . . . Germans?

The Major No, no. <u>Women</u>! Hate Germans, love women.

Polly rises from behind the desk.

Polly What about German women?

The Major . . . Good card players . . .

He wanders off, muttering . . .

Polly shows Basil her phrase book.

Polly Found it.

She heads towards the kitchen with it.

Basil I don't know what you're bothering with that for.

Polly Well they said in the letter that some of them don't speak English.

Basil Well that's their problem, isn't it.

She disappears. Basil goes into his office.

In the office

Basil (*affectionately*) Got her cardy did you? Hmmmm . . . .

In the lobby

Basil comes through, and climbs with the moose onto a chair by the wall where he intends it to hang. The Major emerges from the bar looking at his watch.

The Major By jove, it's nearly six o'clock Fawlty!

Basil Is it?

The Major Yes, well when you're ready I might have a . . . er . . . fruit juice or something.

Basil I'll come and open up the moment I've done this Major.

The Major No immediate hurry . . .

He potters off into the bar.

Basil Drunken old sod.

Basil holds the head up against the wall and starts trying to make a mark with a pencil. The phone starts to ring.

Basil Polly! . . . Polly!! . . . Manuel!!!

*Basil sighs heavily and gets down, carrying
the moose head with him and puts it on
the desk. He picks up the phone.*

Basil Yes Fawlty Towers, yes, hello?

It is Sybil.

Basil I was just doing it you stupid woman! I just put it down to come
here to be reminded by you to do what I'm already doing! I mean,
what's the point of reminding me to do what I'm already doing . . .
I mean <u>what</u> <u>is</u> <u>the</u> <u>bloody</u> <u>point</u>??! I'm doing it aren't I?!!

Sybil has more to say.

Basil Yes I picked it up, yes. No I
haven't had a chance yet, I've been at
it solidly ever since I got back . . . yes
I will, yes. No I haven't yet but I will,
yes. I know it is, yes. I'll try and get it
cleared up, yes all right. Anything
else? I mean would you like the hotel
moved a bit to the left or . . . yes,
well, enjoy the operation dear. Let's
hope nothing goes wrong.

He puts the phone down.

Basil I wish it was an ingrowing tongue

Manuel comes in beaming from the kitchen.

Manuel Yes?

Basil . . . Oh it's the Admirable Crichton. Well?

Manuel You called, sir.

Basil Last week, but not to worry.

Manuel Que?

Basil Oh Buddah. Look, go and get me a hammer.

Manuel Er . . . como?

Basil Hammer.

Pause.

Manuel Oh, hammer sandwich.

Basil Oh, do I have to go through this every time? A hammer!

Manuel My hamster?

Basil No, not your hamster! How can I knock a nail in with your hamster? Well I could try, no it doesn't matter, I'll get it, you come here and tidy, you know, tidy.

Manuel Tidy, si.

Basil strides off towards the kitchen.

Basil I get hhhammmmer and hhhit you on the hhhead with it. Hhhhard . . .

He vanishes. Manuel starts practising his aitches and English phrases . . .

Manuel Hhhhammer. Hello, how are you sir? You see, I speak English well. I learn it from a book. Hello. I am English, hello.

Manuel disappears with his duster below the counter. The Major has come in again from the bar . . .

Manuel's voice How are you, sir.

Manuel's voice I can speak English.

The Major stares. Then he turns away again totally baffled as Manuel appears momentarily above the desk . . .

    Manuel Hello Major. How are you today?

He has disappeared again. The Major turns.

    The Major Er . . . er . . . er . . . fine thank you.

Manuel's voice Is a beautiful day today!

The Major comes slowly towards the moose, peering at it closely.

    The Major Er . . . Is it? Yes, yes, I suppose it is . . .

Manuel's voice I can speak English. I learn it from a book.

The Major . . . Did you? did you really?

*Basil comes back in from the kitchen with
a hammer.*

The Major Ah! There you are Fawlty.

Basil Yes, I'm just going to open up, Major.

*He makes his way to the desk, picks up the
moose, and places it down by the chair. The
Major follows after him.*

The Major Oh, fine . . . er . . .
remarkable animal that Fawlty . . .
where did you get it?

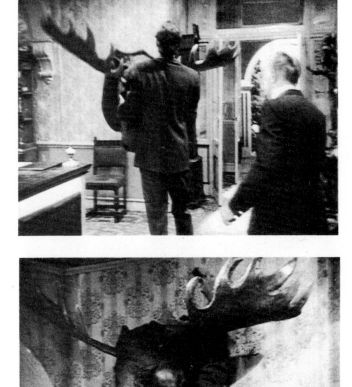

Basil Samson's, in the town.

The Major Really? Was . . . was it expensive?

Basil Er, twelve pounds, I think.

The Major Good Lord! . . .
Japanese was it?

Basil . . . Canadian I think Major.

*Basil knocks in the nail. The Major heads
off to the bar shaking his head . . .*

The Major . . . I didn't know the Canadians were as clever as that.

Basil stares after the departed Major.

Basil . . . He's started early.

*Basil gets down from the chair as Polly
comes into the lobby carrying a vase of
flowers. She takes them to the counter, Basil
looking at them suspiciously.*

Basil Polly? What's that smell?

Polly Flowers. I've just got them from the garden.

Basil Well what are you stinking the place out with those for? What's happened to the plastic ones?

Polly . . . Being ironed.

Basil Coh!

Basil picks up the moose and is about to re-mount the chair when the telephone rings.

Basil Answer that will you Polly? I've got to get this up.

Polly Hello Fawlty Towers? . . . Oh hello Mrs. Fawlty.

Basil (*spinning round*) I'm doing it! I'm doing it now. Tell her, I'm doing it now!

Polly He says he's doing it now . . . yes. How's the nail?

Basil I wish it was this one!

He fixes the moose onto the wall.

Basil There. I've done it. Tell the Tyrant Queen that her cardies are safe forever. Mr. Moose is up. It's done, done, done.

Polly It's up.

Polly It's down.

Basil Give it to me, give it to me . . .

Polly (*to phone*) No, he just fell over Manuel . . . and he seems to have got himself jammed under the swivel chair . . . and the flowers have just fallen on him . . . No, everything else is fine.

Polly rings off.

In reception

The next morning. Basil is replacing the moose. Manuel is in attendance.

Manuel Is up. Good. Very good.

Basil Right. Good.

A long pause.

Basil Well go on, get back to work!

Manuel runs off, stops, and then runs off in another direction, into the kitchen. A couple are coming in the main doors. Basil sees them. They are Mr. and Mrs. Sharp.

Basil Good morning.

Mr. Sharp Good morning.

Basil You know there's a fire drill in a few minutes do you?

Mr. Sharp No, we didn't.

Basil You didn't read the notice.

Mr. Sharp . . . No.

Basil Right, well when you hear the bell, if you'd be so kind as to get out for a few moments, we have to clear the building. Thank you so much.

Mr. Sharp Oh.

As the Sharps leave Polly comes out from the dining room.

Polly Mr. Fawlty, you know it's nearly twelve.

Basil Yes?

Polly Well, the fire drill . . .

Basil (*firmly*) I haven't forgotten, I've just told somebody, I can cope. I mean you know what you're doing do you?

Polly Help get people out of the bedrooms upstairs.

Basil While learning two oriental languages, yes.

Polly Mr. Fawlty?

Basil Yes?

Polly Who else is doing upstairs?

Basil Only you. It doesn't take a moment.

Polly Yes, but I'm only here at mealtimes.

Basil So?

Polly Well, what happens if there's a fire when I'm not here, who does the upstairs then?

Basil . . . We'll worry about that when we come to it shall we? What's the panic? There's always an <u>argument</u> about everything.

The phone rings. Basil picks it up.

Basil Hallo Fawlty Towers . . . Oh what is it <u>now</u>, can't you leave me in peace? . . . Yes, I <u>hadn't</u> forgotten we're just about to <u>have</u> it . . . Yes, I know. I know I need the key, it's on the top . . .

But it isn't.

Basil Well <u>where</u> is it? . . . Well what d'you put it in there for, nobody's going to steal it are they? . . . Yes, I ,know that you know, but I don't do I . . . Yes I do now, thank you so much . . .

He puts the receiver down and goes into the inner office grumbling.

In the office

Basil goes to the safe and starts opening it, still grumbling.

Basil . . . What's she want to put it in the safe for? Always has to complicate everything . . . if I put something down, I know where it is so she goes and moves the damn thing and doesn't tell me . . .

He opens the door of the safe and the burglar alarm goes off. Basil rolls his eyes to heaven.

Basil Well what's she put <u>that</u> on for? Oh, I might have guessed . . .

He goes angrily back into reception.

In reception

The Major has come into the lobby.

Basil Sorry, sorry Major, only the burglar alarm.

Basil drives under the desk and turns off the bell.

The Major What?

Basil Sorry Miss Tibbs!

Miss Tibbs What?

Basil That was the burglar alarm, the fire drill's not for a couple of minutes. Sorry! Excuse me!

The Major Burglars Fawlty?

Basil No, no burglars Major. My wife left the . . . er . . . excuse me!

A large woman has come into the lobby.

Large woman Yes!

Basil That wasn't the fire bell, sorry, that was just the . . . er . . .

Large woman I thought there was a drill?

Basil Yes there is. At twelve o'clock, but not yet.

Large woman But it is twelve o'clock.

Basil Not quite, thank you. Excuse me!

Mr. Sharp Yes?

Large woman Well I make it twelve o'clock.

Basil I'm afraid that that wasn't . . .

Large woman (*to the Major*)
What time do you make it?

Basil Look!

The Major Burglars about I think.

Basil (*getting irritated*) It doesn't matter what time he makes it, it hasn't started yet.

Mr. Sharp What?

Basil It hasn't started yet!

Mrs. Sharp But that was the bell wasn't it?

Basil No!

Large Woman (*to Mrs. Sharp*) He means the drill hasn't started.

Mrs. Sharp What drill? We didn't
hear a drill.

Basil No, no, look, that was the burglar alarm.

The Major See!

Large woman The burglar alarm!

Basil Yes.

Large woman Are there burglars?

The Major Evidently.

Basil Look!! What's the matter with you all? It's perfectly simple. We have the fire drill when I ring the fire bell. That wasn't the fire bell!

Basil Right!??

Mr. Sharp Well how are we supposed to know it wasn't the fire bell?

Basil Because it didn't sound like the fire bell!

All It did.

Basil No it didn't!

All It did.

Basil No it didn't. The firebell is a different . . . it's a semitone higher.

Large woman A <u>semitone</u>?

Basil At least. Anyway the fire drill doesn't start till twelve o'clock.

Mr. Sharp It is twelve o'clock.

Basil . . . Well it is now, but that's because we've been standing around arguing about it!!

Large woman Look, how can you possibly expect us to tell which bell is which? We haven't heard them have we?

Basil You want to hear them? All right. Suits me. Here's the burglar alarm.

He switches it on.

The Major Oughtn't we to catch them first?

Basil There aren't any . . . now <u>listen</u>!!

The Major Well why does the alarm keep going?

Basil All right? Got that? Right!

He turns it off.

Large woman What's happening now?

Basil Now here's the fire bell, right? It's a completely different sound. Listen!

The fire bell starts ringing.

Basil Well where are you going?

Miss. Tibbs Well this is the fire drill isn't it?

Basil No, no, no! This is just so that you can hear the bell so you know what it's like when I do ring it in a moment. Will you come back!! <u>What</u> <u>are</u> <u>you</u> <u>doing</u>? Will you <u>come</u> <u>back</u>??

Miss Tibbs We're going outside!

Basil Not yet! Just listen to it you old fool!

Miss Tibbs (*affronted*) What?

Basil Listen, just listen to it!

At this moment Manuel comes running out of the kitchen, shouting.

Manuel Fire, fire! Everybody out. Please. Fire!

Basil No no!

Manuel Please now out! Out!

Basil Shut up!

Manuel Is fire!!!

Basil Is not fire! Is only bell!

Manuel Que?

Polly runs out from the kitchen and starts to go upstairs.

Basil (*to Polly*) Where are you going?

Polly Upstairs to tell the . . .

Basil There isn't a drill yet! I'm just showing them what the bell sounds like!!

Basil Go in there, go help Chef.

Manuel Chef not here.

Basil Go and . . . start the chips.

Manuel Chips.

Basil Yes. When bell go again . . . stay!

Manuel What?

Basil No fire, only practice. Tell him Polly.

Manuel is successfully despatched to the kitchen. Basil hurries back to the desk.

Basil Thank you, thank you so much ladies and gentlemen, thank you.

The Major Perhaps they're upstairs, Fawlty.

Large woman What is happening now?

Basil Now . . .

He switches off the fire bell, the phone rings . . .

Basil We're having it!!!

He slams the phone down.

Basil Now, if we're all agreed on what the fire bell sounds like we can have the fire drill, which will commence in exactly thirty seconds from now. Thank you so much.

He starts busying himself with papers on the desk. The throng stand around slightly uneasily. Basil looks up at them.

Basil Well, what are you doing? . . . Are you just going to stand there?

Mr. Sharp What do you suggest?

Basil Well couldn't one or two of you go in the bar, and some in the dining room . . . use your imagination a bit?

Large woman Why?

Basil Well this is supposed to be a fire drill!

Mr. Sharp But there's only a few seconds.

Basil Right, right!! Just stay where you are, because obviously if there was a fire you'd all be standing down here in the lobby like this wouldn't you? . . . I don't know why we bother, we should let you all burn . . .

In the kitchen

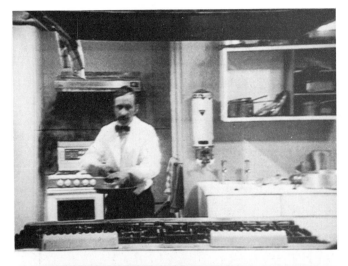

The fire bell goes again.

In reception

People are leaving the hotel in an orderly fashion. Basil is walking with them talking to the Major.

Basil No, there weren't any Major, it went off by accident.

Miss Tibbs Come on, Angina.

Miss Gatsby Thank you, thank you so much.

At this moment Manuel flies out of the kitchen.

Manuel Fire! Fire! Fire!

Basil advances on Manuel.

Basil No! No!

Manuel Si! Si!

Basil Be quiet! Just get on with your work!

He throws Manuel into the kitchen and slams the door. Manuel screams and comes rushing out again.

Manuel Mr. Fawlty! Is fire!

Basil Did you hear what I said?

Manuel No, no, but is fire!!

Basil (*shouting*) Is no fire. Is only bell.

Manuel (*jumping up and down*)
Is fire, is fire, is fire!!

*Basil pushes him into the kitchen. Polly
comes running down the stairs.*

Basil Will you get back in there and stop that!

Manuel (*screaming*) Is fire! Aaaaaaaaaaagh!

*Basil slams the door and turns the key.
Manuel hammers on the door.*

Basil He thinks there's a fire.

Polly Nobody else upstairs.

Manuel is howling.

Polly Manuel! Listen. Listen!! De
nada, de nada, <u>there</u> <u>is</u> <u>no</u> <u>fire</u>!

Polly makes her way behind the reception desk.

Manuel's voice Is fire! Is fire!

*Basil switches off the alarm and pockets
the key. The screaming and hammering
continue from the kitchen.*

Basil Well that'll keep the fire department happy for another six
months. Why we have to bother I don't know.

He leaves by the main doors.

Outside Fawlty Towers

Basil Thank you ladies and
gentlemen, you can come back in
now.

In reception

*Basil walks back into the lobby. Polly is
on the telephone. The noise from Manuel is
terrific.*

Polly Yes, yes, yes, . . . yes, we've
just had it Mrs. Fawlty.

Basil Oh shut up!

Polly Yes, I will, all right, good-bye.

She replaces the receiver and says to Basil . . .

Polly Did you tell Chef about the cheddar?

Large woman Mr. Fawlty, there's an awful row in there!

Basil Yes I know, it's only, oh, I'll deal with it, thank you so much . . .

He strides to the kitchen door and unlocks it.

Basil Now look! I've had enough of this, if you go on I'm . . .

Basil (*loudly*) Excuse me, ladies and gentlemen. Could I have everyone in the lobby?

They all return, complaining and grumbling.

Basil Sorry, sorry. Sorry to disturb you all like this, but . . . there is something that I think I ought to mention. I'm . . . not quite sure how this happened . . . this has not happened at this hotel before, to my knowledge that is, and I'm not sure quite how it's started now . . . er . . .

Large woman What is it?

Basil Well . . . the point is . . . er . . . can I put it this way . . . . fire!

Large woman What?

Basil F-f-f-f-f-f-f-fire!

Mrs. Sharp Fire?

Mr. Sharp Where?

Basil Fire!

Basil Fire!!! Fire!!!

The guests move yet again towards the main doors. Polly has appeared.

Basil What do we do, what do we do?

He rushes to the phone, to call Sybil.

Polly Ring the alarm!

She runs out of the hotel after the guests. Basil dashes hysterically to the alarm. Manuel staggers to the desk in a state of collapse.

Basil . . . . Where's the key?! Where's the key? Would you believe it, I mean would you believe it? The first time we've ever had a fire here in this hotel and somebody's lost the key, I mean isn't that typical of this place . . .

Basil Thank you God, thank you so bloody much!

424

Polly races back.

Polly Smash the glass!

Basil starts hitting the alarm, and injures his hand. He picks up the typewriter to throw it at the glass.

It misses. The phone rings, he snatches the receiver, smashes the glass with it and the bell starts. He then dashes off to get the fire extinguisher, motioning Polly to the kitchen door.

Basil Polly, the door, quick!

He returns with the extinguisher, and starts reading the instructions.

Basil Manuel! Pull it man, Pull it man, Pull it.

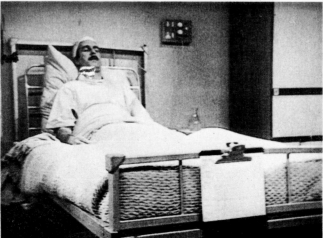

In the Hospital

Basil is lying in bed, re-gaining consciousness with a series of strange noises and expressions. He turns his head and sees Sybil sitting in a wheel chair.

Sybil Well, thank you for coming to see me.

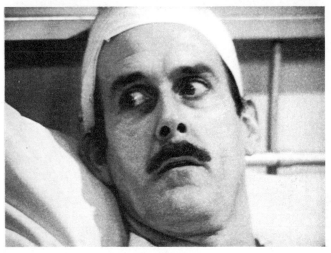

Basil (*very slurred*) Oh not at all, I was just er . . .

Sybil How are you feeling?

Basil . . . The fire!

Sybil It's all . . .

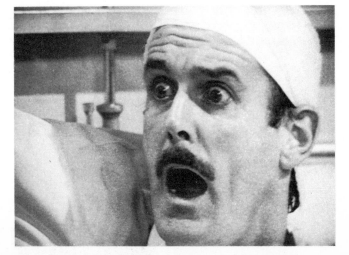

Basil The fire!!

Sybil It's out. There's not much damage . . .

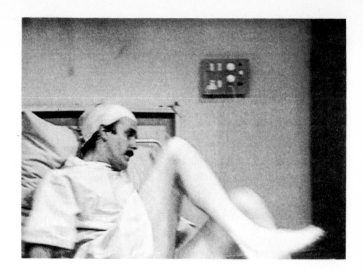

Basil Oh my God, where is it, what have they . . .

Sybil Basil, what are you doing?

Basil . . . Got to get back, got to get back . . .

Sybil Basil! Will you get back into bed!

Basil Tch! Caw! What is it now?

Sybil I'm going to call someone if you don't get back into your bed. Come on!

Basil Listen Sybil, please! I'll handle this if you don't mind. Now . . . what sort of a room do you want?

Sybil Basil!

Basil Oh there you are . . . look, I can't stand round chattering all day, I've got to get back . . .

Sybil Basil you are not well. The doctor says you've got concussion, You must rest.

Basil I'll rest when I get to the hotel.

Sybil I've just spoken to Polly. They're managing perfectly well.

Basil . . . I mean do you know what that fire extinguisher did? It exploded in my face! I mean what is the <u>point</u> of a fire extinguisher? It sits there for months—and when you actually have a fire, when you actually need the bloody thing . . . it blows your head off!! I mean what is happening to this country?! <u>Bloody</u> <u>Wilson</u>!!!

Sister comes in briskly.

Sister . . . My, my, what a lot of noise. Now what are you doing out of your bed?

Basil Going home, thank you so much.

Sister Yes, we'll let the doctor decide that shall we?

She guides the protesting Basil back to bed.

Basil No, let's not.

Sister Come on back to bed.

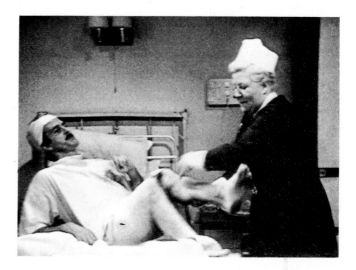

She pushes his legs under the bedclothes.

Basil Don't touch me, I don't know where you've been.

Sister (*smiling indulgently*) Yes we must have our little jokes mustn't we?

Basil Yes we must, mustn't we.

He stares at her very intently . . .

Basil My God, you're ugly aren't you?

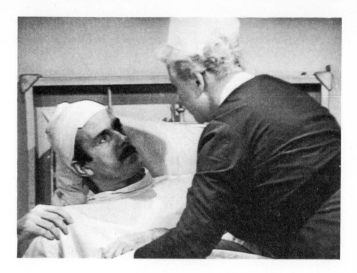

Sybil Basil!

Sister I'll get the doctor.

Sister hurries out of the room. Basil calls after her . . .

Basil You need a plastic surgeon dear, not a doctor!

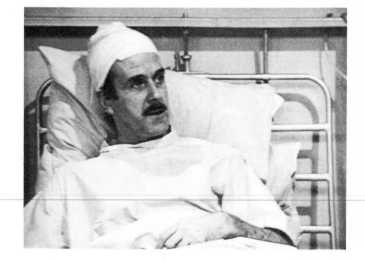

Sybil How dare you talk to sister like that!

Basil gets out again.

Sybil Get back into bed!

Basil You do not seem to realise that I am needed at the hotel!

Sybil No you're not, it's running beautifully without you.

Basil Polly . . . cannot cope!!!

Sybil Well, she can't fall over waiters, or get herself jammed under desks, or start burglar alarms, or lock people in burning rooms, or fire fire extinguishers straight in her own face. But I should think the hotel can do without that sort of coping for a for a couple of days, what do you think Basil . . . hmm?

Basil glares at her sourly. At that moment the doctor comes in and sees his patient . . .

Doctor . . . What?

Basil Oh, hello Doctor.

Doctor Out of bed Mr. Fawlty?

Basil Sort of . . . (*he points vaguely at his slippers on the floor*) Ah! there they are, good! Well, better get back into bed . . . feel a bit woozy.

Doctor You will for a time Mr. Fawlty.

Basil (*obediently*) Yes. Quite, quite.

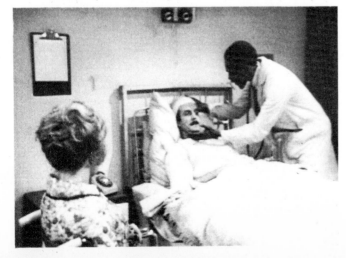

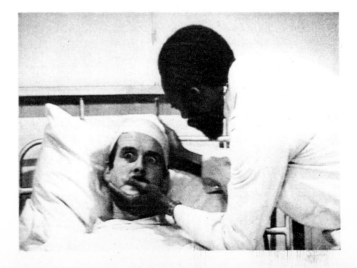

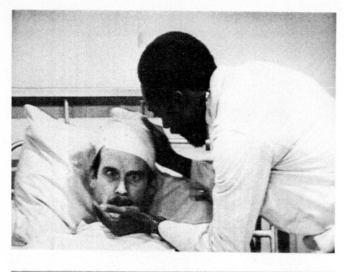
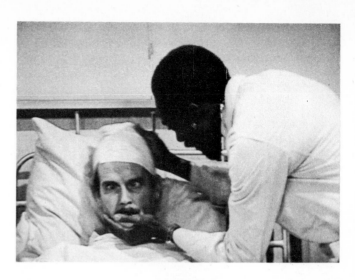

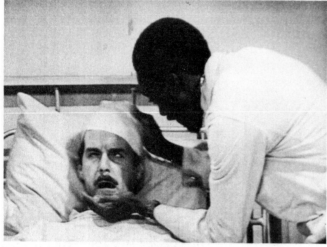
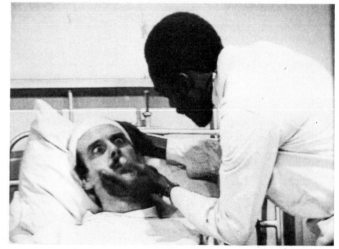

Doctor You should get as much rest as you can . . . as much rest as you can . . .

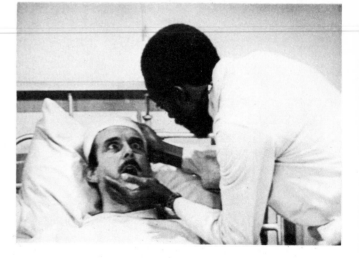

Basil Yes . . . absolutely . . . I er . . . I . . .

Peace. Basil's eyes close. Sybil and the doctor leave the room and close the door gently. Then . . .

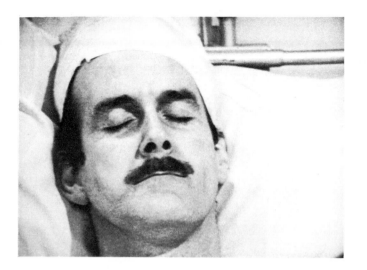 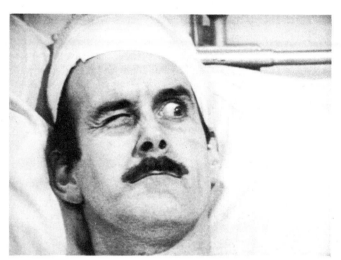

In reception

Polly is finishing a phone call. As she puts the receiver down, a guest approaches the desk, clicks his heels and bows. Polly smiles at him.

    1st German Wann wirt das Mittagessen serviert?

    Polly Um halb eins . . . in funf Minuten.

    1st German Danke schon.

    Polly Bitte schon.

Polly goes into the kitchen, the German guest retires upstairs. Misses Tibbs and Gatsby pass him as they come down to the lobby. Basil enters.

    Basil (*masterfully*) Manuel!

Miss Tibbs Oh, Mr. Fawlty!

Basil Ah, good evening.

Miss Tibbs Are you all right now?

Basil Perfectly thank you.

Basil Take this to my room please dear.

Manuel takes the case, somewhat taken aback.

Miss Gatsby Are you sure you're all right?

Basil Perfectly thank you. Right as rain.

He makes his way a little unsteadily towards the desk, but misses. He re-appears and goes correctly to his position behind the desk. Manuel rushes up.

Manuel You OK?

Basil Fine thank you dear. You go and have a lie-down.

Manuel . . . Que?

Basil Ah, there you are. Would you take my case . . . how did you get that?

Manuel What?

Basil Oh never mind . . . take it . . . take it upstairs!

Manuel (*staring*) . . . I go get Polly!

Basil I've already had one. Take it!

Manuel What?

Basil Take it, take it now . . .

Manuel hurries off.

Basil Tch! The people I have to deal with . . .

He looks up to see a couple approaching the desk. He beams at them . . .

2nd German Sprechen Sie Deutsch?

Basil . . . Beg your pardon?

2nd German Entshuldigen Sie, aber konnen Sie Deutsch sprechen?

Basil . . . . I'm sorry, could you say that again?

3rd German You speak German?

Basil Oh German! I'm sorry, I thought there was something wrong with you. Of course, the Germans!

3rd German You speak German?

Basil Oh . . . er . . . a little . . . I get by.

3rd German Ein bisschen.

2nd German Ah wir . . . wollen . . . ein Auto mieten.

Basil (*nodding helpfully*) Well, why not?

2nd German Bitte.

Basil Yes, a little bit tricky . . . er would you mind saying it again?

3rd German Please?

Basil Could you repeat . . . amplify . . . reiterate? Come on! Yes? Yes?

2nd German . . . <u>Wir</u> . . .

Basil Wir? . . . Yes, well we'll come back to that.

2nd German . . . Wollen . . .

Basil (*to himself*) Vollen . . . Voluntary?

2nd German Ein Auto mieten.

Basil Owtoe . . . out to . . . Oh, I see! You're volunteering to go out to get some meat. Not necessary! <u>We</u> <u>have</u> <u>meat</u> <u>here</u>!

Pause, the couple are puzzled.

Basil (*shouting very loudly*) Vee haff meet hier . . . in ze buildingk!

Basil Moo.

Polly comes in.

Basil Ah Polly, just explaining about the meat.

Polly Oh! We weren't expecting you.

Basil Weren't you? Oh. (*hissing through his teeth*) They're Germans, don't mention the war . . .

Polly I see. (*To Basil*) But Mrs. Fawlty said you were going to rest for a couple of days, you know, in the hospital.

Basil (*firmly*) Idle hands get in the way of the devil's work, Fawlty. Now . . .

Polly Right, well, why don't you have a lie-down, and I can handle this.

Basil Yes, yes. Good idea Elsie. Well done. Bit of a headache actually . . .

Miss Tibbs We don't think you're well Mr. Fawlty.

Basil Well perhaps not, but I'll live longer than you.

Miss Gatsby You must have hurt yourself.

Basil My dear woman, a blow on the head, like that . . . is worth two in the bush.

Miss Tibbs Oh, we know . . . but it was a nasty knock.

Basil Mmmmmm . . . Would you like one?

Basil hits the reception bell impressively.

Basil Next please.

At this moment four more guests come down the stairs.

Basil (*a hoarse whisper*) Polly! Polly! Are these Germans too?

Polly Oh yes, but I can deal . . .

Basil (*urgent and conspiratorial*) Right, right. Here's the plan. I'll stand there and ask them if they want something to drink before their lunch . . . <u>don't</u> <u>mention</u> <u>the</u> <u>war</u>!

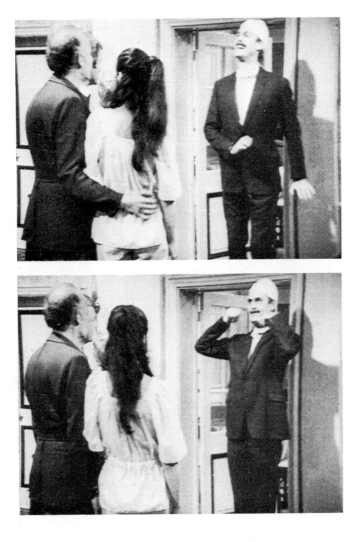

4th German Can we help you?

Basil gives a startled jump.

Basil Ah . . . you speak English.

4th German Of course.

Basil Ah, wonderful. Wunderbar! Ha haaa! Please allow me to introduce myself. I am the owner of Fawlty Towers, and may I welcome your war, you wall, <u>you all</u> . . . and hope your stay will be a happy one. Now, would you like to eat first or would you like a drink before the war . . . <u>ning</u>, that er, trespassers will be tied up with piano wire.

Basil Aah! Sorry! Sorry!

Basil Bit of trouble with the old leg. Bit of shrapnel in the war . . . <u>Korean</u>, Korean War, sorry, Korean.

4th German Thank you, we will eat now.

Basil bows graciously and ushers the party into the dining room.

Basil Oh good, please do allow me. This way. May I say how delighted I am to have some Europeans here now that we are all on the Continent . . .

They all go in.

Polly May I speak to Dr. Fin please?

In the dining room

Basil is taking the orders.

Basil I didn't vote for it myself quite honestly, but now that we're in I'm determined to make it work, so I'd like to welcome you all to Britain. The plaice is grilled, but that doesn't matter, there's life in the old thing yet . . . Now wait a moment, I got a bit confused there. Oh yes, the plaice is grilled . . . in fact the whole room's getting a bit hot isn't it? I'll open a window, have a look . . . And the veal chop is done with rosemary . . . . . . that's funny, I thought she'd gone to Canada . . . and is delicious and nutricious . . . ha, ha, in fact it's <u>veally</u> good. Ha, ha, <u>veally</u> good.

1st German The veal is good?

Basil Yes, doesn't matter, never mind.

1st German May we have two eggs mayonnaises please?

Basil Certainly, why not?
We are all friends now, eh?

4th German (*heavily*) A prawn cocktail . . .

Basil . . . All in the Market together, old differences forgotten, and no need at all to mention the war.

Basil Sorry!!

Basil I'm sorry, what was that again?

4th German A prawn cocktail.

Basil Oh prawn, ah that was it. When you said <u>prawn</u> I thought you said war. Oh yes the war! It completely slipped my mind, I'd forgotten all about it. Hitler, Himmler, and all that lot. I'd completely forgotten it, just like that!

He snaps his fingers.

Basil . . . Sorry, what was it again?

4th German (*with some menace*) A prawn cocktail . . .

Basil Oh yes, Eva prawn . . .

Basil And Goebbels of course, he's
another one I can hardly remember at all.

5th German And ein <u>pickled</u> <u>herring</u>!

Basil Hermann Goering, yes, yes . . . and von Ribbentrop, that was
another one.

4th German And four cold meat salads please.

Basil Certainly, well I'll just get your hors d'oeuvres, . . . d'oeuvres
vich of course must be obeyed at all times vithout question. Sorry!
Sorry!!

Polly Mr. Fawlty, will you call your
wife immediately?

Basil Sybil!! . . . Sybil!! . . . . . . she's
in the hospital you silly girl!

Polly Yes, call her there!

Basil I can't, I've got too much to do. Listen, listen! (*He whispers through his teeth*) Don't mention the war.

Basil ... <u>I</u> mentioned it once, but I think I got away with it ...

He returns to his guests.

Basil ... Anyway it's all forgotten now and let's not hear any more about it.

Basil So ... that's two egg mayonnaise, a prawn Goebbels, a Hermann Goering and four Colditz salads ... wait a minute, I got a bit confused here, sorry ...

One of the German ladies has begun to sob.

Basil I got a bit confused because everyone keeps mentioning the war, so could you please ...

Basil What's the matter?

4th German It's all right.

Basil Is something wrong?

4th German Will you please stop talking about the war?

Basil Me? You started it!

4th German We did not start it.

Basil Yes you did, you invaded Poland.

Basil offers her a napkin.

> **Basil** Here, have a blow. Look, this'll cheer you up, you'll like this one, there's this woman, she's completely stupid . . . can never remember anything and her husband's in a bomber over Berlin . . .

The lady howls.

> **Basil** Sorry! Sorry! Here, here she'll love this one . . .

> **4th German** Oh stop, will you leave her alone?

> **Basil** No, this one's a scream, I've never seen anyone not laugh at this!

> **1st German** (*shouts*) Go away!

Basil Look, she'll love it. She's German!!

Polly No, Mr. Fawlty!!

Basil Do Jimmy Cagney.

Basil Who?

Polly Jimmy Cagney!

Basil Jimmy Cagney?

Polly You know . . . 'You dirty rat . . .'

Basil I can't <u>do</u> Jimmy Cagney.

Polly Please try . . . 'I'm going to get you . . .'

Basil Shut up! Here, watch!

Basil Who's this then?

He does his Fuhrer party piece. The audience is stunned.

Basil I'll do the funny walk . . .

Both Germans Stop it!!!

Basil What? I'm trying to cheer her
up you stupid Kraut!

4th German It's not funny for her.

Basil Not funny?? You're joking!

4th German Not funny for her,
not for us, not for any German people.

A pause.

Basil (*quite amazed*) You have absolutely no sense of humour, do you!

1st German (*shouting*) It is not funny!

Basil . . . Who won the bloody war anyway??

Doctor Mr. Fawlty, you'll be all right.

Basil Fine.

Suddenly he dashes off through the kitchen, out across the lobby and into the office. He spots the medical men in pursuit and leaves by the other door back into reception . . .

In reception

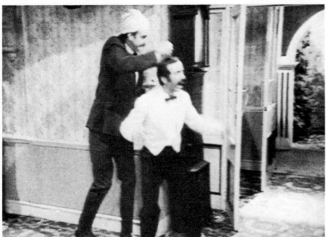

Basil is knocked cold. The moose's head lands on Manuel. The Major, entering from the bar, is intrigued.

Manuel's voice Oooooh, my head!
He hit me on the head . . .

The Major No, <u>you</u> hit <u>him</u> on the
head. You <u>naughty</u> moose!

4th German However did they win?